100% NEW
DEVELOPING MAT

CW00369648

**Photocopiable
teaching resources
for mathematics**

COUNTING AND UNDERSTANDING NUMBER

Ages 10–11

**Hilary Koll and
Steve Mills**

A & C Black • London

Contents

Find the difference between a positive and negative integer, or two negative integers, in context

Use decimal notation for tenths, hundredths and thousandths; partition, round and order decimals with up to three places, and position them on the number line

Express a larger whole number as a fraction of a smaller one; simplify fractions by cancelling common factors; order a set of fractions by converting them to fractions with a common denominator

Express one quantity as a percentage of another; find equivalent percentages, decimals and fractions

Solve simple problems involving direct proportion by scaling quantities up or down

Published 2008 by A & C Black Publishers Limited
38 Soho Square, London W1D 3HB
www.acblack.com

ISBN 978-0-7136-8447-6

Copyright text © Hilary Koll and Steve Mills 2008
Copyright illustrations © KJA Artists 2008
Copyright cover illustration © Piers Baker 2008
Editors: Lynne Williamson and Marie Lister
Designed by HL Studios, Oxford

The authors and publishers would like to thank Catherine Yemm and Corinne McCrum for their advice in producing this series of books.

A CIP catalogue record for this book is available from the British Library.

Printed and bound in Great Britain by Martins the Printers, Berwick-on-Tweed.

A & C Black uses paper produced with elemental chlorine-free pulp, harvested from managed sustainable forests.

Introduction

All New Developing Numeracy: Counting and Understanding Number is a series of seven photocopiable activity books for Key Stages 1 and 2 designed to be used during the daily maths lesson. The books focus on the skills and concepts for Counting and Understanding Number as outlined in the National Strategy's Primary Framework for literacy and mathematics. The activities are intended to be used in the time allocated to pupil activities; they aim to reinforce the knowledge and develop the facts, skills and understanding explored during the main part of the lesson and to provide practice and consolidation of the objectives contained in the Framework document.

Counting and Understanding Number

This strand of the *Primary Framework for mathematics* is concerned with helping pupils to develop and understanding of the relationships between numbers and the way our number system works. It includes all aspects of counting, ordering, estimating and place value and involves building awareness of how numbers can form sequences and can be represented on number lines and in grids. Also included in this strand of the curriculum is work on negative numbers, fractions, decimals, percentages and ratio and proportion. Broadly speaking, this strand addresses topic areas that were described under the 'Numbers and the Number System' strand title of the former National Numeracy Strategy's *Framework for teaching mathematics*.

Counting and Understanding Number Ages 10–11

supports the teaching of mathematics by providing a series of activities to develop essential skills in counting and recognising numbers. The following objectives are covered:

- find the difference between a positive and a negative integer, or two negative integers, in context;
- use decimal notation for tenths, hundredths and thousandths; partition, round and order decimals with up to three places, and position them on the number line;
- express a larger whole number as a fraction of a smaller one, e.g. recognise that 8 slices of a 5-slice pizza represents $\frac{8}{5}$ or $1\frac{3}{5}$ pizzas; simplify fractions by cancelling common factors; order a set of fractions by converting them to fractions with a common denominator;
- express one quantity as a percentage of another, e.g. express £400 as a percentage of £1000; find.equivalent percentages, decimals and fractions;
- solve simple problems involving direct proportion by scaling quantities up or down.

Extension

Many of the activity sheets end with a challenge (**Now try this!**) which reinforces and extend children's learning, and provides the teacher with an opportunity for assessment. These might include harder questions, with numbers from a higher range, than those in the main part of the activity sheet. Some extension activities are open-ended questions and provide opportunity for children to think mathematically for themselves. Occasionally the extension activity will require additional paper or for children to write on the reverse of the sheet itself. Many of the activities encourage children to generate their own questions or puzzles for a friend to solve.

Organisation

Very little equipment is needed, but it will be useful to have the following resources available: coloured pencils, counters, cubes, scissors, glue, coins, squared paper, number lines, grids and tracks.

Where possible, children's work should be supported by ICT equipment, such as number lines and tracks on interactive whiteboards, or computer software for comparing and ordering numbers. It is also vital that children's experiences are introduced in real-life contexts and through practical activities. The teachers' notes at the foot of each page and the more detailed notes on pages 6 to 11 suggest ways in which this can be effectively done.

To help teachers select appropriate learning experiences for the children, the activities are grouped into sections within the book. However, the activities are not expected to be used in this order unless stated otherwise. The sheets are intended to support, rather than direct, the teacher's planning.

Some activities can be made easier or more challenging by masking or substituting numbers. You may wish to re-use pages by copying them onto card and laminating them.

Accompanying CD

The enclosed CD-ROM contains electronic versions of all the activity sheets in the book for printing, editing, saving or display on an interactive whiteboard. Our unique browser-based interface makes it easy to select pages and to modify them to suit individual pupils' needs. See page 12 for further details.

Teachers' notes

Brief notes are provided at the foot of each page, giving ideas and suggestions for maximising the effectiveness of the activity sheets. These can be masked before copying.

Further explanations of the activities can be found on pages 6 to 11, together with examples of questions that you can ask.

Whole class warm-up activities

The tools provided in A & C Black's Maths Skills and Practice CD-ROMs can be used as introductory activities for use with the whole class. In the Maths Skills and Practice CD-ROM 6 the following activities and games could be used to introduce or reinforce 'Counting and Understanding Number' objectives:

- Jumbo d'Hut
- Lolly Hunt
- Dove Dudes
- Guess.imals
- Beat the Boss
- Pet Percents

The following activities provide some practical ideas that can be used to introduce or reinforce the main teaching part of the lesson, or to provide an interesting basis for discussion.

Run-around fractions

Around the walls of the hall or classroom, pin pieces of paper showing a variety of fractions. Ask the children to stand in the middle of the room and call out a fraction that is equivalent to one around the room. Ask them to find this fraction and run to the correct sign. This can be played as a game where children who are standing by incorrect signs are out. Variations on this activity include calling out:

- a number and asking children to find a fraction with that denominator or numerator;
- a fraction question such as, 'Which fraction is half of one fifth?' or 'Which fraction is one quarter more than one half?'

Run-around decimals

Around the walls of the hall or classroom, pin pieces of paper showing whole numbers between 1 and 10. Ask the children to stand in the middle of the room and call out a decimal. Ask them to round this decimal to the nearest whole number and run to the correct sign. This can be played as a game where children who are standing by incorrect signs are out. Variations on this activity include calling out:

- a decimal that is equivalent to a fraction or percentage on the wall;
- a percentage that is equivalent to a fraction or decimal on the wall.

Fraction and ratio features

Invite some children to the front of the class and pick a feature that some of them have, e.g. brown hair or wearing a skirt. Invite the rest of the class to say what fraction of the set of children have this feature e.g. 'three eighths of the children are wearing a tie' or 'four tenths of the children are girls'. Ask them then to describe the feature as a ratio, e.g. 'there are three children wearing a tie for every 5 children who are not' or 'the ratio of girls to boys is 4 to 6'. Where a ratio can be given as a simpler equivalent, such as 4 to 6 as 2 to 3, encourage the children in the set to get into identical groups to show this, e.g. two groups each with 2 girls to every 3 boys.

Constant function

The constant function facility on a calculator is a useful way of exploring decimals sequences and sequences that extend backward beyond zero to include negative numbers. Ask children to explore the patterns produced on a calculator by pressing these buttons (checking with the calculator manual if necessary).

5 + + 0.2 = = = = = = etc.
10 - - 0.1 = = = = = = etc.
1.2 + + 0.3 = = = = = = = etc.
3.1 - - 0.5 = = = = = = etc.

Once children have become familiar with the patterns created, one child can stand at the front of the class with the calculator and the class can begin to count in decimal-sized steps. The child with the calculator must check for mistakes.

Notes on the activities

Find the difference between a positive and negative integer, or two negative integers, in context

Counting forwards and backwards in different-sized steps to zero is a vital part of repeated addition and early multiplication and helps children to begin to recognise and memorise multiplication facts. Counting on and back from any number in different-sized steps helps children to build up an awareness of where numbers are in relation to each other. At this age, children are developing a sense of awareness about how decimals and fractions relate to each other as shown on number lines. Counting backwards beyond zero is an important step in developing an understanding of negative integers and their relationships with each other. Encourage the children to use number lines and grids to help them to explore such sequences, and to look for patterns in the digits, which will help them to become more effective in recognising and explaining sequences.

The manhunters! (page 13)

Children could use the constant function on a calculator to help them check the numbers they generate in these sequences. Begin by keying in the start number followed by the subtraction sign twice and the number on the bride, such as 10 – – 6 (on most calculators). By continuing to press the = key the display will show the numbers in the sequence.

SUGGESTED QUESTIONS:

- Which number comes next?
- How do you know?
- How could you check your answers?

Going hot and cold (page 14)

You may prefer to write in a range of negative numbers before copying, rather than allowing the children to write their own. The children can check their answers with a calculator. Ask them to key in the negative number and either add (for temperature rises) or subtract (for temperature falls) the number of degrees in the question.

SUGGESTED QUESTIONS:

- Is this a temperature rise or fall? Is the number of degrees going to get bigger or smaller?
- Is ⁻5 °C hotter or colder than ⁻6 °C?

Rollercoaster ride (page 15)

Encourage the children to tackle this activity several times to practise moving up and down between negative and positive integers. They should record the numbers as a trail of numbers on a separate sheet of paper, for example: ⁻5, ⁻3, 4, ⁻1, 6, 0, ⁻9, ⁻5, ⁻2, ⁻7. Once the trails have been written, the children can then look at them and begin to identify the size of the steps between the adjacent numbers, for instance, from ⁻5 to ⁻3 is a step of 2, from ⁻3 to 4 is a step of 7.

SUGGESTED QUESTIONS:

- What is the size of the step from ⁻5 to 7?
- How many down do you go to get from 1 to ⁻4?

Time travel (page 16)

As a further extension activity, you could ask children to work out what day of the week ⁻1, +10, ⁻7, +3 etc. would be if day 0 is 'today'.

SUGGESTED QUESTIONS:

- I am in the day ⁻1. If I travel forwards for 6 days in time, which day do I reach?
- I am in the day 3. If I travel backwards for 10 days in time, which day do I reach?

Time zones (page 17)

This sheet can also be used to practise telling the time in different places, for example, If the time in London (0) is 16:30, what is the time in Anchorage/Sydney? The children could also use atlases to find the time zones of countries not marked on the activity sheet.

SUGGESTED QUESTIONS:

- How many hours further on is Sydney than Cape Town? How could you work this out?
- What is the difference between ⁻5 and 2?

Mount Everest (page 18)

To emphasise that a difference is always given as a positive number, display a large number line and use a piece of string to show that the 'distance' between 3 and 5 is the same as between ⁻3 and ⁻5 and ⁻2 and 0, and ⁻1 and 1.

SUGGESTED QUESTIONS:

- How much do you think the temperature outside today has varied?
- What do you think the temperature outside today might be?

Fly me to the moon (page 19)

Explain that a difference is not negative, but rather always positive and that it just represents how far apart two numbers or temperatures are.

SUGGESTED QUESTION:

- What is the temperature difference between these two temperatures?

I am the champion (page 20)

To check the children's work, ask them to record their turns into a table, like this:

First number	Second number	Difference
⁻17	23	40

The children could also check their answers using a number line or calculator. They could also draw their own grids and write their own positive and negative integers to create more games.

SUGGESTED QUESTIONS:

- Which is the smallest number in your opponent's grid?
- How many more is ⁻3 than ⁻5?

Use decimal notation for tenths, hundredths and thousandths; partition, round and order decimals with up to three places, and position them on the number line

The ability to partition numbers and decimals that are written in figures relies heavily on an understanding of place value, that is, an understanding that the position of a digit determines its value. For example the 7 in 41·73 represents 7 tenths (0·7), whereas the 7 in 745 400 represents 7 hundred thousands (700 000). If children have not fully grasped this concept then they are likely to confuse numbers like 4·305 with 4·035 and so on.

In order to be confident with adding and subtracting numbers, the children need to be aware that numbers can be partitioned (split) in many different ways, particularly into multiples of 1000, 100, 10 and 1 and so on, for example, that 35·48 is 30 + 5 + 0·4 + 0·08 or 30 + 4 + 1·4 + 0·08 or 30 + 5 + 0·3 + 0·18.

Decimal game and Decimal game cards: 1 and 2 (pages 21, 22 and 23)

The cards can be used for a whole range of purposes in addition to the activity on these pages. They could be used to help the children to order decimals, find those that total 1, partition them or to say and write the names of numbers in words. They can also be arranged with addition and equals signs to make number statements such as 0·03 + 0·17 = 0·2. The decimals on the cards could also be used for converting into percentages and fractions.

SUGGESTED QUESTIONS:

- What number are you on at the moment?
- How many more do you need to reach the number 1?
- Can you find two cards that have a total of 0·5?

At full stretch (page 24)

It is simple to make these expanding numbers using strips of thin paper or card. Write the number in the expanded form and fold up the paper so that only the digits of the contracted form can be seen.

This is a useful classroom resource. A template can be made without digits and then laminated. New digits can then be written onto the plastic and wiped off to create a more flexible resource.

SUGGESTED QUESTIONS:

- Which is the largest/smallest number? Write these in first.
- How many hundredths/thousandths has this number?

Snowflakes (page 25)

All the numbers in the snowflakes could be masked before copying and the children could make up their own snowflake sequences, counting on and back in tenths, hundredths or thousandths.

SUGGESTED QUESTIONS:

- Is this sequence increasing or decreasing?
- How many tenths more is this number?
- What is one thousandth more than 3·261?

Crocodile snap!: 1 and 2 (pages 26 and 27)

This activity shows whether children understand the place value of decimals. If children struggle with this activity it might be useful for them to partition each number into parts to help them appreciate the different digit values, for example 43·73 = 40 + 3 + 0·7 + 0·03 and 16·7 = 10 + 6 + 0·7, so the 7 tenths is in both numbers.

SUGGESTED QUESTIONS:

- How would you say this number?
- What is the value of the digit 5 in this number?
- How many thousandths has this number?
- Which of these decimals is larger?

Decimal partitions (page 28)

Partitioning in different ways, using multiples of hundreds, tens and ones or when using decimals, underpins the most commonly-used method of subtraction known as decomposition. When subtracting 15·9 from 38·1 using a written method the 38·1 can be changed to 3 tens, 7 ones and 11 tenths so that the 9 tenths in 15·9 can be subtracted. Partitioning in this way can help the children to appreciate what is happening when the numbers are being crossed out and exchanged.

SUGGESTED QUESTION:

- The pattern is moving one hundredth across each time. What will the next number in the pattern be?

Banana drama (page 29)

It can be helpful for the children to make all the decimals have the same number of decimal places by putting zeros into the hundredths or thousandths column, for example writing 7·340 or 7·500 rather than 7·34 and 7·5 which makes it easier to decide where to place a decimal such as 7·409.

SUGGESTED QUESTIONS:

- Which is the smallest number in this list? How do you know?
- How many tenths has it?
- How many hundredths?

Weighty questions (page 30)

Encourage children to compare the numbers by looking at the most significant digits first, in this case the units, then the tenths, hundredths and finally the thousandths. This should help them to remember the decreasing value of the digits.

SUGGESTED QUESTIONS:

How do you know that 3·099 is less than 3·55?
Where would the number 3·264 belong in this list? How do you know?

Coconut shy (page 31)

At the start of the lesson, practise counting in steps of 0·1, 0·01 and 0·001 from different start numbers.

SUGGESTED QUESTION:

• Is this going up in steps of one tenth or one hundredth?

Decimal puzzle: 1, 2 and 3 (pages 32, 33 and 34)

These sheets are at three levels of difficulty. Children will require scissors and glue for this activity. Provide each child with a sheet and ask them to fit the small hexagons into the centres of the larger ones so that each decimal has been correctly rounded. If necessary, to make these activities a little simpler, ask the children to start with the larger hexagons and to round each decimal to the nearest whole number/tenth/hundredth. The answers can be written in the centre of the large hexagons. The children can then find the matching small hexagons showing the same numbers.

SUGGESTED QUESTIONS:

• How would you round this decimal to the nearest whole number/tenth/hundredth?

Express a larger whole number as a fraction of a smaller one (for example, recognise that 8 slices of 5-slice pizza represents $\frac{8}{5}$ or $1\frac{3}{5}$ pizzas); simplify fractions by cancelling common factors; order a set of fractions by converting them to fractions with a common denominator

Children of this age should appreciate the role of the denominator and numerator in a fraction for determining how many equal parts something has been split into, and how many are being described. They should be confident in finding equivalents by multiplying or dividing the numerator and denominator by the same number.

It is also important that children begin to appreciate that mixed numbers lie between whole numbers on number lines. Counting forwards and backwards can help the children to gain an appreciation of how fractions and mixed numbers relate to whole numbers and to each other.

Pack it in (page 35)

At the start of the lesson, revise the meanings of 'improper fraction', 'mixed number', 'denominator' and 'numerator'. Check that children understand that the phrase 'what fraction of a 6-pack of yoghurt is 7 pots?' means 'what fraction do we write when we have 7 lots of one-sixth?'

SUGGESTED QUESTIONS:

What fraction of a 6-pack of yoghurts is 5 pots?

How is that fraction different to all your answers on the page?

How are we related? (page 36)

This activity is good to play as a classroom activity, once children are confident in expressing one number as a fraction of another. Give each child in the room a number card to hold. Ask the children to move around the room and, as they meet people, to say what fraction of the other person's number their own is, for example: 'My number is $\frac{9}{10}$ of your number' or 'My number is $1\frac{1}{9}$ times your number'. To assist the children with this skill, point out that their number will always be the numerator and the other child's number will be the denominator. If their number is larger, they should try to convert the improper fraction to a mixed number.

SUGGESTED QUESTIONS:

• What fraction of £10 is £4?
• What fraction of £4 is £10? How could you say this as a mixed number?

Fraction quiz (page 37)

Ensure the children appreciate that there may be more than one correct answer for the quiz questions.

SUGGESTED QUESTION/PROMPT:

• Show me how you worked that out.
• What fraction of the whole week is the weekend?

A sure measure (page 38)

In this activity, the children have to express their answers in the simplest form. Before they complete the questions on the worksheet, practise simplifying proper fractions, for example $\frac{35}{70}$, $\frac{28}{100}$ and $\frac{63}{72}$.

SUGGESTED QUESTIONS:

• How could you simplify this fraction further?
• What is this improper fraction as a mixed number?

Domino loop (page 39)

These dominoes could be enlarged onto A3, copied and then laminated for a more permanent resource.

SUGGESTED QUESTIONS:

• What is this improper fraction as a mixed number?
• What is the denominator of this number?
• How many fifths are there in one-whole/two-wholes?

Robot twins (page 40)

Check that the children simplify the fractions to the smallest denominator possible. For some of the fractions (for example $\frac{5}{20}$, $\frac{18}{54}$, $\frac{36}{48}$ and $\frac{45}{90}$), it is possible to divide the denominator by the numerator.

SUGGESTED QUESTIONS:

- Which number did you divide the numerator and the denominator by?
- Is there another number you could divide them by?
- Which times-table contains the numbers 12 and 32?
- What is the highest common factor of 45 and 90?

I scream for ice-cream (page 41)

The extension activity asks the children to find fractions of 40 and then simplify the result. As a further extension, the children can investigate what happens when they find what fraction of 80 or 120 each number is.

SUGGESTED QUESTIONS:

- Which number did you divide the numerator and the denominator by?
- Is there another number you could divide them by?
- Is this fraction in its simplest form?

Colour by fractions (page 42)

As a means of checking their answers, the children could be asked to write all the fractions into the groups 'yellow', 'red', 'blue', 'orange' and 'green'. These can then be checked against the answers at the back of this book.

SUGGESTED QUESTIONS:

- Which number did you divide the numerator and the denominator by?
- Is there another number you could divide them by?

Fraction line-up (page 43)

At the start of the lesson, demonstrate how the numerator and the denominator of each fraction can be multiplied by a number so that all of the equivalent fractions have the same denominator.

SUGGESTED QUESTIONS:

- Have you multiplied or divided both the numerator and the denominator by the same number here?
- Are these two fractions equivalent? Which has been written with smaller numbers?
- Do all your equivalent fractions now have the same denominator?

Fraction friends (page 44)

As a further extension, the children could write another equivalent fraction for each set in the main activity.

SUGGESTED QUESTIONS:

- Do all your equivalent fractions now have the same denominator?
- How does this approach help us to order fractions?
- Is there another way that we could check our answers?

Fraction spell (page 45)

As a further extension, the children could check their answers using a calculator. Show them how the fractions can be converted to decimals by dividing the numerator by the denominator, and then the decimals compared.

SUGGESTED QUESTIONS:

- Do all your equivalent fractions now have the same denominator?
- How does this approach help us to order fractions?
- Is there another way that we could check our answers?

Telly addict (page 46)

At the start of the lesson, ask the children to list all the pairs of factors of 60. Discuss how this list can help them find equivalents with the denominator 60 of the fractions in the main activity.

SUGGESTED QUESTIONS:

- How do you know that $\frac{24}{60}$ is equivalent to $\frac{2}{5}$?
- $\frac{11}{15}$ is equivalent to $\frac{44}{60}$, so what is $\frac{13}{15}$ equivalent to?

Express one quantity as a percentage of another (for example express £400 as a percentage of £1000); find equivalent percentages, decimals and fractions

> Understanding the relationship between decimals, fractions and percentages is an important part of later mathematics work. From an early age, children encounter fractions, decimals and percentages in everyday life, but need to refine their understanding of what is meant by them and how they relate to each other.
>
> Appreciating that one-tenth can be written as $\frac{1}{10}$ or 0·1 or 10% is often accepted easily by children, but accepting that $\frac{1}{2}$ = 0·5 = 50% is more difficult. It is vital that children have an understanding of equivalent fractions so that they can see that $\frac{1}{2}$ is equivalent to $\frac{5}{10}$ and thus is written as 0·5, and that $\frac{1}{2}$ is equivalent to $\frac{50}{100}$ and therefore equivalent to 50%.

Top that!: 1 and 2 (pages 47–48)

These worksheets could be enlarged on a photocopier, stuck onto card, coloured and laminated for a more permanent classroom resource. Children find this kind of trumping game very entertaining once they are comfortable with the rules. It allows them to compare numbers (comparing two numbers if two play, three numbers if three play, and so on).

This specific set of cards is useful for helping children to recognise that larger percentages do not necessarily mean more overall. For example, discuss that 7·7% of Chinese people are aged 65+ and 11·7% of people in Iceland are aged 65+, however, since there are so many more people altogether in China, the total number of people of this age in China is more than in Iceland.

These cards can also be used for further investigation, for example more confident children could use the population figures on the cards to calculate the number of men and women in each country, or find the number of people of different ages.

SUGGESTED QUESTIONS:

- What did you like best about the game?
- Can we make some more 'Top that!' cards to use?

Percentage code (page 49)

This activity can help children to appreciate that more than one fraction can convert to the same percentage. In this activity, several different fractions convert to 24%. Draw the children's attention to this fact once the worksheet is completed. As an extension, ask the children to make up their own percentage code for a partner to solve.

SUGGESTED QUESTIONS/PROMPT:

- What number do you need to multiply by to go from 20 to 100?
- Now multiply the numerator by this number.
- How would you write this fraction as a percentage?

gBay (page 50)

At the start of the lesson, check that the children understand what is meant by the percentage rating, and why sellers and buyers might find it useful. Would they want to buy from someone with a rating of 23%?

SUGGESTED QUESTIONS:

- How could you work out different scores that would give a rating of 85%?
- Can you explain to a partner what you would do?

Cat and mouse (page 51)

This activity can help children to begin to recognise fractions, decimals and percentages of the same value, without the need to work out the equivalents.

SUGGESTED QUESTIONS:

- Which fraction is equivalent to 0·6?
- What is the value of the digit to the right of the decimal point?
- How do you convert a decimal into a percentage?

Hoopla stall (page 52)

Tell the children that they should be drawing exactly 29 hoops on this worksheet to encourage them to persist in finding all the equivalents. Encourage them to discuss how they might solve these problems. Some children might like to write each percentage as a fraction with a denominator of 100, and then find which fractions are equivalent to this one. Alternatively, the children could convert each given fraction to a percentage, using a calculator if necessary.

SUGGESTED QUESTIONS:

- How do you know that that fraction is equivalent to that percentage?
- What do you notice about all the fractions that are equivalent to that percentage?

Colour it! (page 53)

This type of question is a common context used in the National Tests for 11 year olds.

SUGGESTED QUESTIONS:

- How did you work out how many percent that part was of the whole shape?
- If I colour purple half of what is unshaded, what percentage would be left unshaded?

Dragon's labyrinth (page 54)

For this activity, encourage the children to record their trails on a separate piece of paper and to use only percentages in their trails. As an extension, the children could try to find routes that give:

a. the lowest total

b. the total 78%

c. the total nearest to 100%.

SUGGESTED QUESTIONS:

- Can you find a trail with a total close to 60%?
- What is $\frac{1}{25}$ as a percentage?

Virus alert! (page 55)

This activity is useful for assessing the children's understanding of percentages and their relationship to fractions and decimals.

SUGGESTED QUESTION/PROMPT:

- Write two sentences like these about the percentage 93%.
- What percentage is equivalent to $\frac{7}{20}$?

Clever conversions (page 56)

If you would prefer to provide specific fractions, decimals or percentages for this activity, write one number into each row of the tables. You might choose to give only fractions, or you might choose to provide a mixture of fractions, decimals or percentages.

$\frac{1}{2}$	0·5	50%	$\frac{9}{10}$	0·9	90%
$\frac{1}{4}$	0·25	25%	$\frac{3}{20}$	0·15	15%
$\frac{3}{4}$	0·75	75%	$\frac{1}{50}$	0·02	2%
$\frac{1}{10}$	0·1	10%	$\frac{7}{10}$	0·7	70%
$\frac{1}{5}$	0·2	20%	$\frac{24}{25}$	0·96	96%
$\frac{3}{5}$	0·6	60%	$\frac{4}{5}$	0·8	80%
$\frac{1}{100}$	0·01	1%	$\frac{53}{100}$	0·53	53%
$\frac{3}{25}$	0·12	12%	$\frac{34}{50}$	0·68	68%
$\frac{1}{20}$	0·05	5%	$\frac{17}{20}$	0·85	85%
$\frac{17}{100}$	0·17	17%	$\frac{2}{5}$	0·4	40%
$\frac{7}{25}$	0·28	28%	$\frac{7}{100}$	0·07	7%

SUGGESTED QUESTIONS/PROMPT:

- Explain to me how you found out that $\frac{3}{20}$ is equivalent to 0·15.
- If you didn't have a calculator, how could you work this out?
- Could you change the fraction to a percentage first?

Solve simple problems involving direct proportion by scaling quantities up or down

Ratio and proportion are closely related topics, but their differences must be clearly understood. Ratio compares part with part, for example '3 red beads for every 2 yellow beads', whereas proportion compares the part with the whole, for example '3 red beads in every 5 beads'. Proportions are usually described as fractions but can also be shown as decimals or percentages.

When a quantity gets larger or smaller, it is said to change. Sometimes a change in one quantity causes a change, or is linked to a change, in another quantity. If these changes happen in the same ratio, then the quantities are said to be in direct proportion, such as the number of pizzas and the cost of them: two pizzas cost £7.00 and five cost £17.50. The more you buy, the more they cost.

To be certain whether two things are in direct proportion you can divide one quantity by the other for each pair of values. This will always give the same answer, for example £7 ÷ 2 = £3.50, £17.5 ÷ 5 = £3.50. At this age, children are beginning to appreciate the multiplicative nature of direct proportional situations and should be encouraged to see how numbers can be scaled up and down, for example how the cost of one pizza or four pizzas can be found using the original information.

Hens and chicks (page 57)

Encourage the children to cover the unused part of the ratio diagram with a book or hand when they are answering the questions.

SUGGESTED QUESTIONS:

- How many chicks are in the yard if there are 24 hens?
- How could you work this out quickly without using the diagram?

Spoon it out (page 58)

Before beginning the activity, check that the children know the difference between a teaspoon and a tablespoon. This activity can help children to understand direct proportion ideas. Ask them to look for the patterns in the numbers – this will help the children to begin to see the sequences in the numbers and to predict new sets of groups.

SUGGESTED QUESTION:

- Can you see how the answers relate to your times-tables?

'Coven' Garden Market (page 59)

Remind the children to look at whether the prices are given in pounds or pence to ensure that they give the correct unit in their answers.

SUGGESTED QUESTIONS:

- How much will five spider webs cost if two cost 60p?
- Which of these calculations did you find most difficult? Why?

Great grams (page 60)

This activity involves children scaling up or down to solve direct proportion questions. Encourage the children to discuss the methods that could be used to solve this type of problem, for example they could find the cost per gram and then multiply, or they could work out the fraction of 100 g (for example $2\frac{1}{2}$ times larger) and then multiply the price accordingly. Give the children the opportunity to try a variety of methods and to say which approach they prefer.

SUGGESTED PROMPT:

- Show me how you worked out how many grams were bought.

Are we nearly there? (page 61)

Some children might find it useful to draw marks on the diagram to show the relative distances. For example for question 1, they might want to divide the distance from A to B in two so that they can see that to find the distance AB, they have to divide 60 km by three and then double the result.

SUGGESTED QUESTION:

- Can you explain to us how you worked out these answers?

Cooking crisis (page 62)

In this activity, the children should use the times-table facts that they know for numbers to 10 × 10 to help them first divide three-digit numbers by one-digit numbers, and then multiply multiples of 10 by one-digit numbers.

SUGGESTED QUESTIONS/PROMPT:

- Explain how you worked out how much cream was needed for the soup for nine people.
- Would you need more or less beef if you were making Beef Baldaire for nine people? How much more?

Using the CD-ROM

The PC CD-ROM included with this book contains an easy-to-use software program that allows you to print out pages from the book, to view them (e.g. on an interactive whiteboard) or to customise the activities to suit the needs of your pupils.

Getting started
It's easy to run the software. Simply insert the CD-ROM into your CD drive and the disk should autorun and launch the interface in your web browser.

If the disk does not autorun, open 'My Computer' and select the CD drive, then open the file 'start.html'.

Please note: this CD-ROM is designed for use on a PC. It will also run on most Apple Macintosh computers in Safari however, due to the differences between Mac and PC fonts, you may experience some unavoidable variations in the typography and page layouts of the activity sheets.

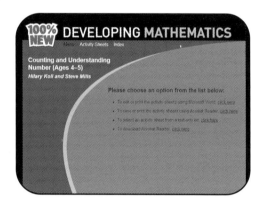

The Menu screen
Four options are available to you from the main menu screen.

The first option takes you to the Activity Sheets screen, where you can choose an activity sheet to edit or print out using Microsoft Word.

(If you do not have the Microsoft Office suite, you might like to consider using OpenOffice instead. This is a multi-platform and multi-lingual office suite, and an 'open-source' project. It is compatible with all other major office suites, and the product is free to download, use and distribute. The homepage for OpenOffice on the Internet is: www.openoffice.org.)

The second option on the main menu screen opens a PDF file of the entire book using Adobe Reader (see below). This format is ideal for printing out copies of the activity sheets or for displaying them, for example on an interactive whiteboard.

The third option allows you to choose a page to edit from a text-only list of the activity sheets, as an alternative to the graphical interface on the Activity Sheets screen.

Adobe Reader is free to download and to use. If it is not already installed on your computer, the fourth link takes you to the download page on the Adobe website.

You can also navigate directly to any of the three screens at any time by using the tabs at the top.

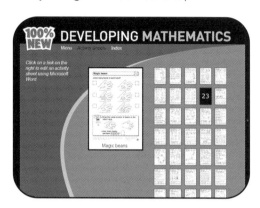

The Activity Sheets screen
This screen shows thumbnails of all the activity sheets in the book. Rolling the mouse over a thumbnail highlights the page number and also brings up a preview image of the page.

Click on the thumbnail to open a version of the page in Microsoft Word (or an equivalent software program, see above.) The full range of editing tools are available to you here to customise the page to suit the needs of your particular pupils. You can print out copies of the page or save a copy of your edited version onto your computer.

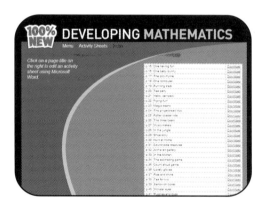

The Index screen
This is a text-only version of the Activity Sheets screen described above. Choose an activity sheet and click on the 'download' link to open a version of the page in Microsoft Word to edit or print out.

Technical support
If you have any questions regarding the *100% New Developing Literacy* or *Developing Mathematics* software, please email us at the address below. We will get back to you as quickly as possible.

educationalsales@acblack.com

The manhunters!

- Help each bride to find her man!
- On the bride is the number you count back in.
- Draw the trail from each bride in a different colour.

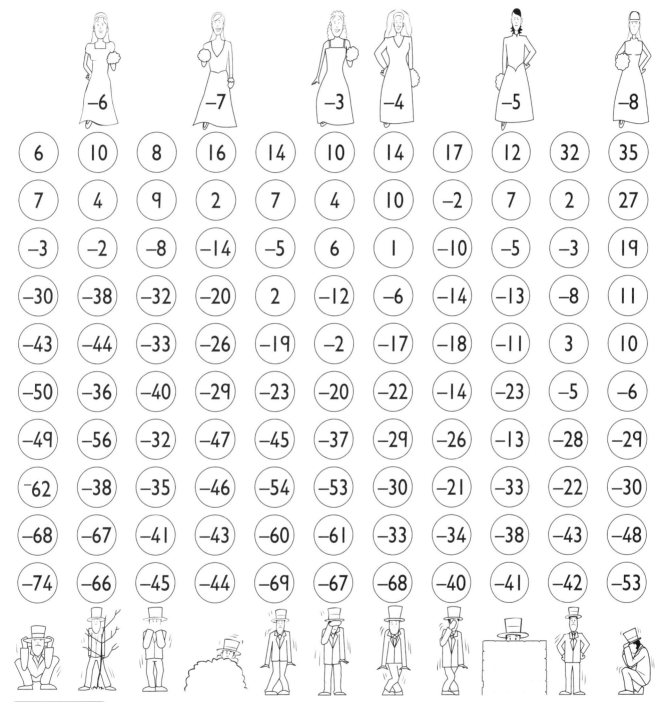

Teachers' note Children will need coloured pencils or pens for this activity.

100% New Developing Mathematics
Counting and Understanding
Number: Ages 10–11
© A & C BLACK

13

Going hot and cold

- **Fill in each box with numbers between ⁻1 and ⁻10.**
- **Write the new temperature each time.**
- **Use the number line to help you.**

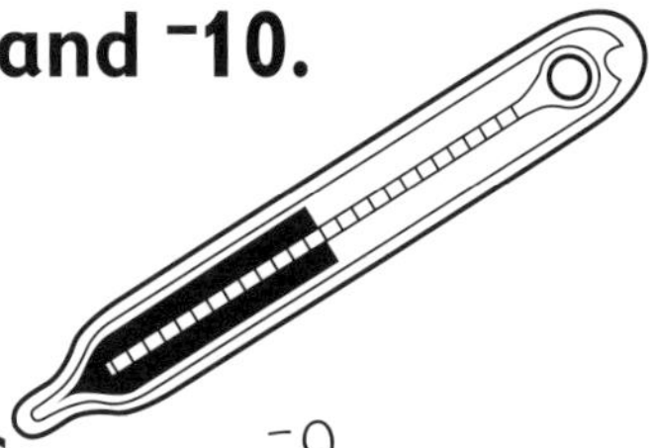

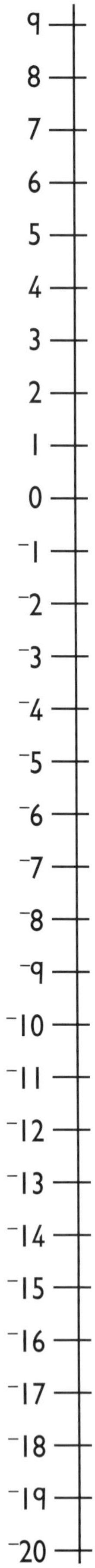

1 It was [⁻2] °C. The temperature **fell** by 7 °C.   ___⁻9___

2 It was [ ] °C. The temperature **rose** by 11 °C.   _____

3 It was [ ] °C. The temperature **fell** by 9 °C.   _____

4 It was [ ] °C. The temperature **rose** by 8 °C.   _____

5 It was [ ] °C. The temperature **fell** by 5 °C.   _____

6 It was [ ] °C. The temperature **rose** by 12 °C.   _____

7 It was [ ] °C. The temperature **fell** by 6 °C.   _____

8 It was [ ] °C. The temperature **rose** by 4 °C.   _____

9 It was [ ] °C. The temperature **fell** by 8 °C.   _____

10 It was [ ] °C. The temperature **rose** by 14 °C.   _____

11 It was [ ] °C. The temperature **fell** by 11 °C.   _____

12 It was [ ] °C. The temperature **rose** by 13 °C.   _____

NOW TRY THIS!

- **Write ten pairs of temperatures with a difference of 18 °C. Use positive and negative numbers.**

Number line (right side):
9, 8, 7, 6, 5, 4, 3, 2, 1, 0, ⁻1, ⁻2, ⁻3, ⁻4, ⁻5, ⁻6, ⁻7, ⁻8, ⁻9, ⁻10, ⁻11, ⁻12, ⁻13, ⁻14, ⁻15, ⁻16, ⁻17, ⁻18, ⁻19, ⁻20

Teachers' note This activity can be used to help the children to appreciate the sizes of gaps between positive and negative numbers and can be used as an introduction to finding the differences between positive and negative integers. Remind the children that when temperatures fall and it gets colder, the size of the digits in the temperatures may get bigger.

100% New Developing Mathematics
Counting and Understanding
Number: Ages 10–11
© A & C BLACK

Rollercoaster ride

☆ Choose a number between zero and ⁻10 as your starting number.
☆ Write this number down.
☆ Roll a dice and move along the rollercoaster.
☆ As you land on a section follow the instructions.
☆ Write down each number in your number trail.
☆ Do this several times.

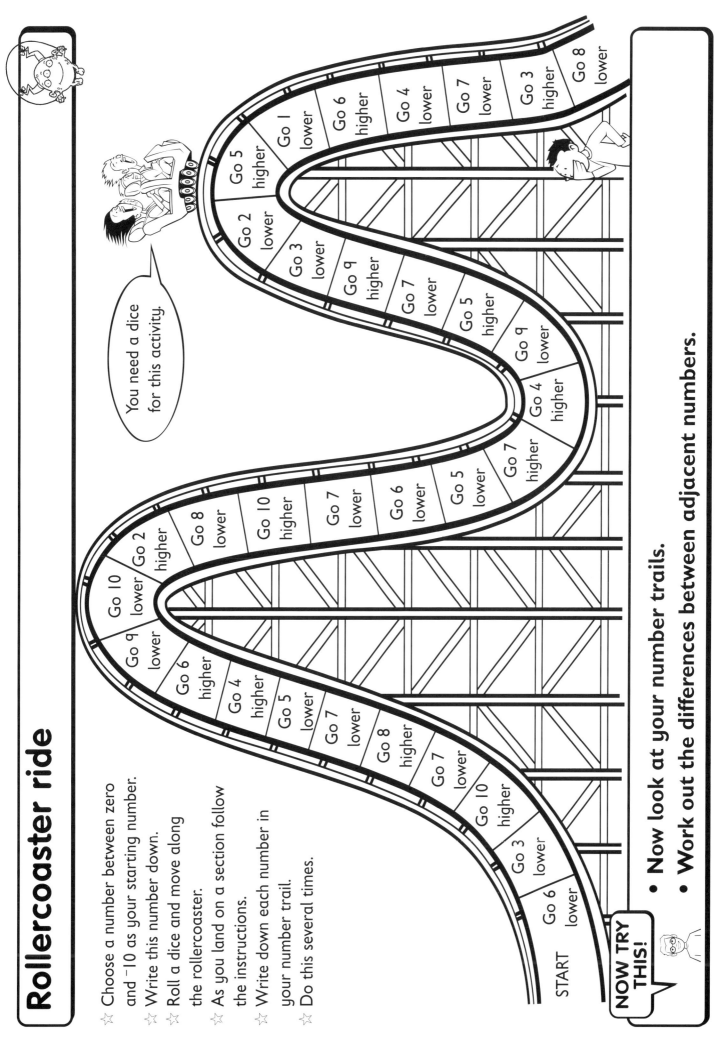

You need a dice for this activity.

Go 5 higher
Go 1 lower
Go 6 higher
Go 4 lower
Go 7 lower
Go 3 higher
Go 8 lower

Go 2 lower
Go 3 lower
Go 9 higher
Go 7 lower
Go 5 higher
Go 9 lower
Go 4 higher
Go 7 higher
Go 5 lower
Go 6 lower
Go 7 lower
Go 10 higher
Go 8 lower
Go 2 higher
Go 10 lower
Go 9 lower
Go 6 higher
Go 4 higher
Go 5 lower
Go 7 lower
Go 8 higher
Go 7 lower
Go 10 higher
Go 3 lower
Go 6 lower

START

NOW TRY THIS!

• Now look at your number trails.
• Work out the differences between adjacent numbers.

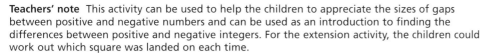

Teachers' note This activity can be used to help the children to appreciate the sizes of gaps between positive and negative numbers and can be used as an introduction to finding the differences between positive and negative integers. For the extension activity, the children could work out which square was landed on each time.

100% New Developing Mathematics
Counting and Understanding
Number: Ages 10–11
© A & C BLACK

Time travel

A magic time-travel machine is able to travel forwards and backwards in time. If it goes back one day in time from the day zero, the day would be called ‾1 and so on.

- **Play this game with a partner. You each need different-coloured pencils.**

☆ Take turns to roll two dice and choose in which direction to move the time-travel machine that many days. Mark its new position by circling the number.

☆ Continue playing in this way.

☆ The winner is the player who brings the machine back to zero.

NOW TRY THIS!

- **Write ten statements to show the differences between the days you have circled, like this:**

  The difference between the days ‾3 and 7 is 10.

Teachers' note At the start of the lesson call out a time traveller's journey by giving a trail of instructions and ask the children to follow the trail on the number line above, for example, go back 4 days, go forward 7 days, go back 9 days, go forward 10 days, and so on. Encourage the children to say the day aloud, such as negative four, negative five etc.

100% New Developing Mathematics
Counting and Understanding
Number: Ages 10–11
© A & C BLACK

Time zones

This map shows some time differences around the world.
The positive or negative numbers show how many hours in
front or behind London, England, each place is.

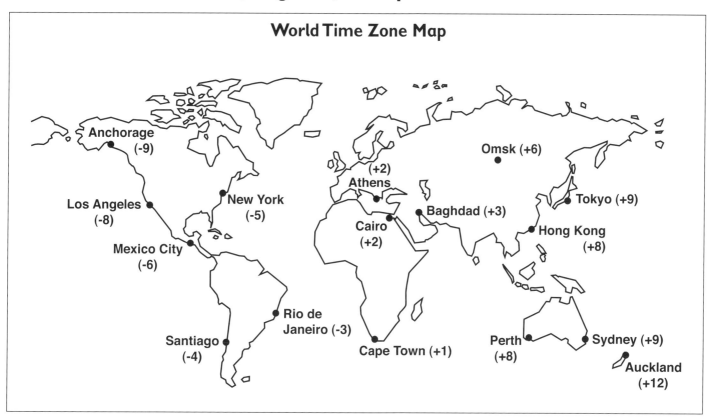

World Time Zone Map

Anchorage (-9)

Los Angeles (-8)

New York (-5)

Mexico City (-6)

Santiago (-4)

Rio de Janeiro (-3)

Cape Town (+1)

Athens (+2)

Cairo (+2)

Baghdad (+3)

Omsk (+6)

Tokyo (+9)

Hong Kong (+8)

Perth (+8)

Sydney (+9)

Auckland (+12)

- ## How many hours in front of:

  1 New York is Cairo? _7_

  2 Santiago is Hong Kong? ____

  3 Athens is Tokyo? ____

  4 Anchorage is Mexico City? ____

  5 Los Angeles is Perth? ____

  6 Baghdad is Sydney? ____

  7 Rio de Janeiro is Omsk? ____

  8 Anchorage is Tokyo? ____

  9 Mexico City is Cape Town? ____

  10 New York is Auckland? ____

  11 Anchorage is Omsk? ____

  12 Los Angeles is Hong Kong? ____

  13 Santiago is Sydney? ____

  14 Rio de Janeiro is Perth? ____

NOW TRY THIS!

- **Write ten statements about the time differences between these, or other places around the world.**

Teachers' note At the start of the lesson discuss the children's experiences, if any, of time zones. Explain how this map shows the times around the world in relation to Greenwich, London, where +3 means three hours in front and ⁻7 means 7 hours behind. Demonstrate how to calculate the time differences between pairs of places.

100% New Developing Mathematics
Counting and Understanding
Number: Ages 10–11
© A & C BLACK

Mount Everest

The data in this table shows the maximum and minimum temperatures in summer and in winter at the **Everest Base Camp** and at the **summit**.

	Everest Base Camp	The summit
Summer maximum	25 °C	⁻5 °C
Summer minimum	⁻9 °C	⁻40 °C
Winter maximum	10 °C	⁻19 °C
Winter minimum	⁻30 °C	⁻50 °C

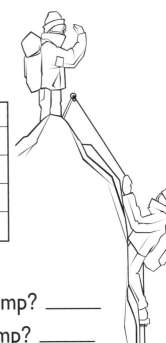

1 How many degrees colder is the:

   a summer maximum at the summit than at Base Camp? _____

   b summer minimum at the summit than at Base Camp? _____

   c winter maximum at the summit than at Base Camp? _____

   d winter minimum at the summit than at Base Camp? _____

2 At Everest Base Camp, how many degrees colder is the:

   a winter maximum than the summer maximum? _____

   b winter minimum than the summer minimum? _____

   c summer minimum than the summer maximum? _____

   d winter minimum than the winter maximum? _____

3 At the summit, how many degrees colder is the:

   a winter maximum than the summer maximum? _____

   b winter minimum than the summer minimum? _____

   c summer minimum than the summer maximum? _____

   d winter minimum than the winter maximum? _____

NOW TRY THIS!

- **Which location has the largest difference in temperature between its summer high and its winter low?** _____
- **What is this difference?** _____

Teachers' note Explain that a difference is not negative, but rather always positive and that it just represents how far apart two numbers or temperatures are.

100% New Developing Mathematics
Counting and Understanding
Number: Ages 10–11
© A & C BLACK

Fly me to the moon

The moon, unlike Earth, does not have an atmosphere so temperatures vary a lot over its surface. Some scientists have placed probes to measure the temperatures at different points on the moon.

	Station 1	Station 2	Station 3	Station 4	Station 5
Night	⁻150 °C	⁻122 °C	⁻100 °C	⁻96 °C	⁻120 °C
Day	90 °C	⁻3 °C	80 °C	⁻96 °C	⁻10 °C

	Station 6	Station 7	Station 8	Station 9	Station 10
Night	⁻170 °C	⁻125 °C	⁻166 °C	⁻157 °C	⁻184 °C
Day	170 °C	0 °C	152 °C	120 °C	214 °C

1 What is the difference between night and day temperatures at:

a Station 7? _125 °C_   **b** Station 3? _____   **c** Station 1? _____

d Station 6? _____   **e** Station 5? _____   **f** Station 4? _____

g Station 2? _____   **h** Station 10? _____   **i** Station 8? _____

j Station 9? _____

2 Which station's temperature varies:

a the most? _____   **b** the least? _____

3 Find the temperature difference at night between:

a Stations 7 and 3 _____   **b** Stations 3 and 5 _____

c Stations 1 and 10 _____   **d** Stations 6 and 4 _____

e Stations 5 and 2 _____   **f** Stations 2 and 8 _____

g Stations 9 and 1 _____   **h** Stations 10 and 4 _____

NOW TRY THIS!

- **Find stations with a day temperature difference of:**

100 °C   186 °C   173 °C   86 °C   248 °C   310 °C

Teachers' note It could be explained to the children that Station 4 is positioned at one of the poles of the moon, where the temperature remains constant and that Station 10, where the temperature range is largest, is at a point on the 'equator'.

100% New Developing Mathematics
Counting and Understanding
Number: Ages 10–11
© A & C BLACK

I am the champion

• Play this game with a partner.

☆ The aim of the game is to 'destroy' all your opponent's 'defences'. Player 1 picks two of player 2's numbers and says the difference between them. If they are correct, they cross out those two numbers, 'destroying' them. The winner is the first to have destroyed their opponent's defences.

☆ Play two games.

Game 1

Player 1

-3	-22	30	-58	18	-12
-8	-31	7	-27	0	10

Player 2

-33	91	17	-10	-50	-2
23	0	-28	80	-25	-9

Game 2

Player 1

-1	-19	33	-49	-8	-27
17	-11	-17	-53	9	32

Player 2

-39	18	-25	-16	-54	-9
38	-2	-41	-18	-25	4

NOW TRY THIS!

• **Now write ten pairs of positive and negative numbers with a difference of 17.**

Teachers' note Suggest that the child with the shortest first name goes first in game 1 and then swap for game 2 to make it fairer. Give the children a negative number line to check the differences and encourage them to use zero as a stopover when finding the difference between a positive and negative number.

100% New Developing Mathematics
Counting and Understanding
Number: Ages 10–11
© A & C BLACK

Decimal game

- **Play this game in groups of 2, 3 or 4. You each need a copy of this sheet and the cards cut from Decimal game cards: 1 and 2.**

☆ Place the cards face down on the table.

☆ Begin at zero on the first number line on your sheet.

☆ Take turns to pick (and keep) a card and move forward that many.

☆ Mark your new position with a cross and write its decimal.

☆ Score points according to the key.

☆ If you pick a card that takes you **above** 1, miss a turn.

☆ The winner is the player with the most points when someone has reached 1 or when all the cards are used.

☆ Start a new game on the next number line.

Key

Score points if you land on:

$\frac{1}{2}$	**6 points**
$\frac{1}{4}$ or $\frac{3}{4}$	**5 points**
0·1, 0·2, 0·3, 0·4, 0·6, … 0·9	**4 points**
a number with 5 hundredths (e.g. 0·05)	**3 points**
The first person to land on 1 exactly	**5 points**

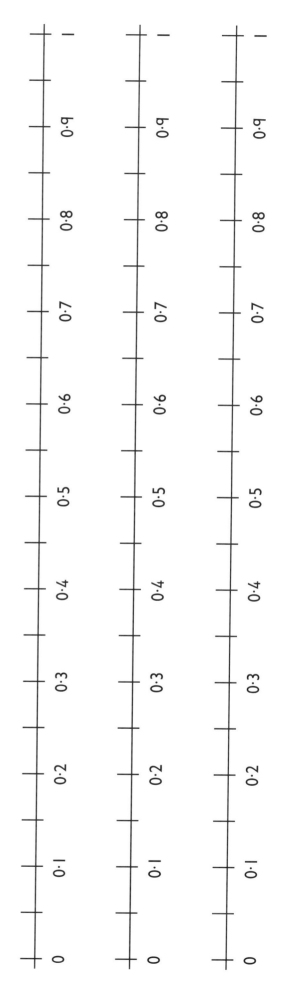

Teachers' note Enlarge the sheet to A3 when copying.

**100% New Developing Mathematics
Counting and Understanding
Number: Ages 10–11**
© A & C BLACK

Decimal game cards: 1

0·03	**0·12**	**0·17**
0·05	**0·18**	**0·15**
0·01	**0·19**	**0·14**
0·06	**0·09**	**0·04**
0·4	**0·1**	**0·2**
0·3	**0·1**	**0·2**
0·02	**0·08**	**0·05**
0·04	**0·07**	**0·03**

Teachers' note Use this page in conjunction with pages 21 and 23. For alternative uses for these cards, see page 6.

100% New Developing Mathematics
Counting and Understanding
Number: Ages 10–11
© A & C BLACK

0·01	0·11	0·13
0·05	0·16	0·17
0·09	0·21	0·22
0·24	0·09	0·23
0·25	0·26	0·27
0·28	0·29	0·25
0·02	0·08	0·05
0·04	0·07	0·03

Teachers' note Use this page in conjunction with pages 21 and 22. For alternative uses for these cards, see page 6.

100% New Developing Mathematics
Counting and Understanding
Number: Ages 10–11
© A & C BLACK

23

At full stretch

This decimal is being expanded.

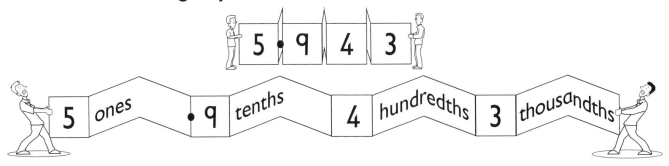

- **Fill in the missing numbers.**

1

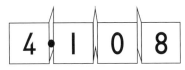

8	thousandths		tenths
	ones		hundredths

2

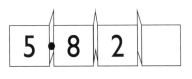

	hundredths		tenths
	thousandths		ones

3

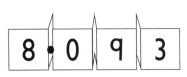

	thousandths		hundredths
	tenths		ones

4

	ones		thousandths
	hundredths		tenths

NOW TRY THIS!

- **Circle which of these decimals show 5 thousandths.**

  5·205   55·25   0·055   50·551

  5·002   52·5   25·255   0·505

Teachers' note At the start of the lesson, ask the children to write decimals to three places and invite them to read the numbers to the rest of the class.

100% New Developing Mathematics
Counting and Understanding
Number: Ages 10–11
© A & C BLACK

Snowflakes

Each line of decimals forms a sequence.

- Continue the sequences and fill in the missing decimals.

3·216

3·207

3·217

3·117

3·257

3·229

3·258 3·239

3·459

3·059

2·458

3·061

2·455

2·457

2·661

Teachers' note Encourage the children to describe each sequence using the words tenths, hundredths or thousandths, for example, this sequence is increasing in steps of 2 tenths each time, or this goes up in steps of one thousandth. As an extension activity, ask the children to find six pairs of numbers in the snowflakes that have a difference of 1.

100% New Developing Mathematics
Counting and Understanding
Number: Ages 10–11
© A & C BLACK

- **Cut out the cards and play 'snap' with a partner.**

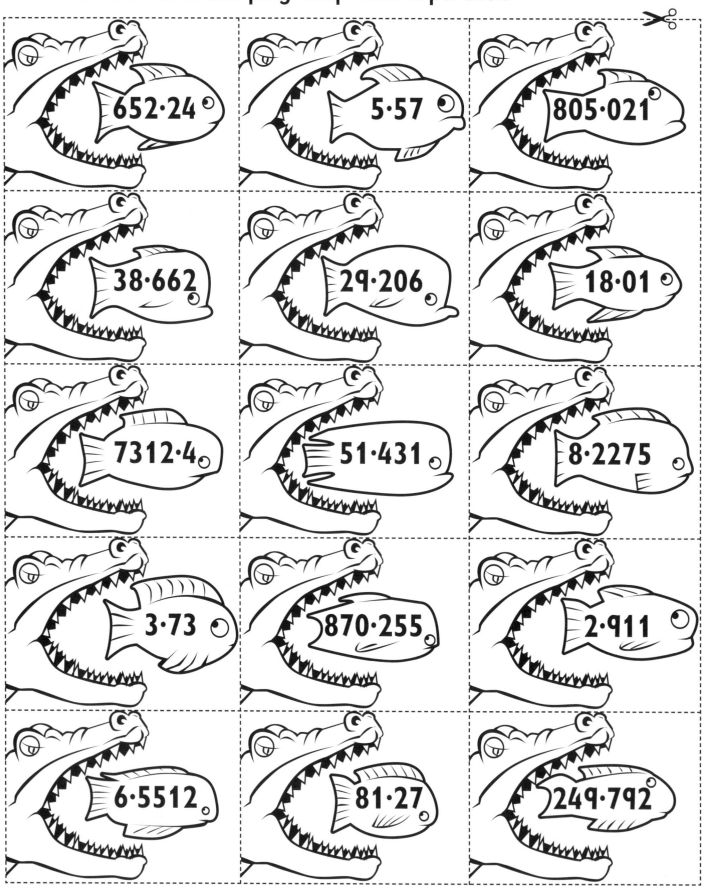

652·24

5·57

805·021

38·662

29·206

18·01

7312·4

51·431

8·2275

3·73

870·255

2·911

6·5512

81·27

249·792

Teachers' note This sheet should be used in conjunction with page 27.

26

100% New Developing Mathematics
Counting and Understanding
Number: Ages 10–11
© A & C BLACK

• **Cut out the cards and play 'snap' with a partner.**

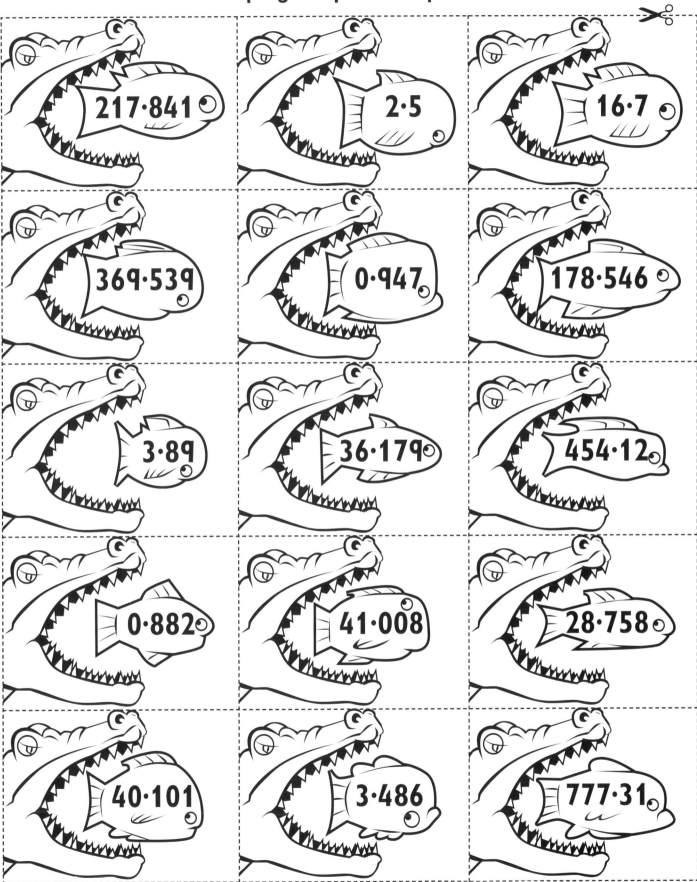

Teachers' note Each child has a pile of 15 cards. Children should say 'snap' when two numbers have any digits in common. They must read the numbers aloud and say the value of the common digit to win the cards. Alternatively, ask each child to turn over two cards. If the numbers have a digit that is worth the same amount they should write the value of the digit that is the same.

100% New Developing Mathematics
Counting and Understanding
Number: Ages 10–11
© A & C BLACK

Decimal partitions

• **Partition the decimal in different ways, continuing the patterns.**

8·671

8	+	0·6	+	0·07	+	0·001
8	+	0·6	+	0·06	+	0·011
8	+	0·6	+	0·05	+	0·021
8	+	0·6	+	_____	+	_____
8	+	_____	+	_____	+	_____
8	+	_____				

8·671

8	+	0·6	+	0·07	+	0·001
8	+	0·5	+	0·17	+	0·001
8	+	0·4	+	_____	+	_____
8	+	0·3	+	_____	+	_____
8	+	_____	+	_____	+	_____
8	+	_____				

8·671

8	+	0·6	+	0·07	+	0·001
7	+	1·6	+	0·07	+	0·001
6	+	_____	+	_____	+	_____
5	+	_____	+	_____		
		_____	+	_____		
		_____	+	_____		

9·458

9	+	0·4	+	0·05	+	0·008
9	+	0·4	+	0·04	+	0·018
9	+	_____	+	_____	+	_____
9	+	_____	+	_____		
		_____	+	_____		
		_____	+	_____		

9·458

9	+	0·4	+	0·05	+	0·008
9	+	0·3	+	0·15	+	0·008
9	+	_____	+	_____	+	_____
9	+	_____				
9	+	_____				

9·458

9	+	0·4	+	0·05	+	0·008
8	+	1·4	+	_____	+	_____
7	+	_____	+	_____	+	_____
6	+	_____	+	_____		
5	+	_____				

NOW TRY THIS!

• **Make up a number with a unit and three decimal places.**
• **Write your own partition patterns, like those above.**

Teachers' note This skill is valuable for helping the children to understand written methods of addition and subtraction. It is particularly useful as a way to assist them with the decomposition method of subtraction. Encourage the children to look closely to see how the number is being partitioned and to check each answer by adding. They could also use a calculator to check answers.

100% New Developing Mathematics
Counting and Understanding
Number: Ages 10–11
© A & C BLACK

Banana drama

- **Write the decimals in each bunch in order, with the smallest first.**

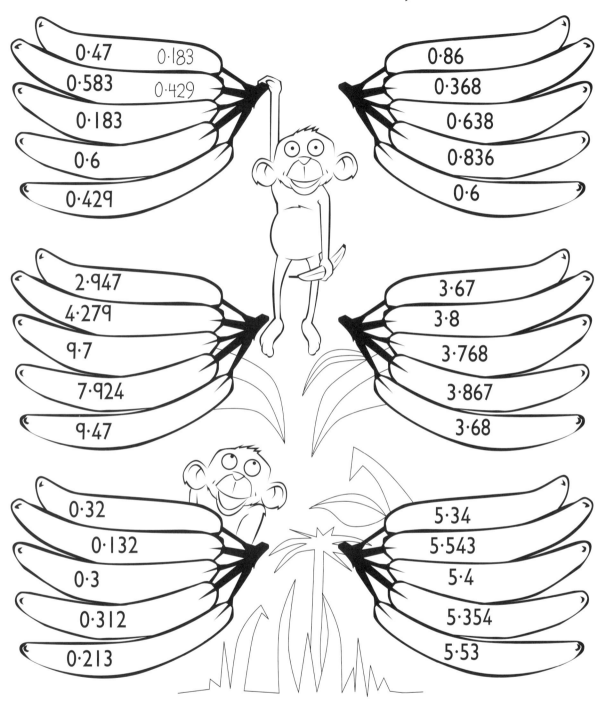

0·47 0·183
0·583 0·429
0·183
0·6
0·429

0·86
0·368
0·638
0·836
0·6

2·947
4·279
9·7
7·924
9·47

3·67
3·8
3·768
3·867
3·68

0·32
0·132
0·3
0·312
0·213

5·34
5·543
5·4
5·354
5·53

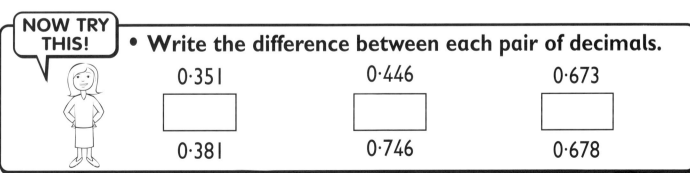

NOW TRY THIS!

- **Write the difference between each pair of decimals.**

0·351	0·446	0·673
0·381	0·746	0·678

Teachers' note At the start of the lesson revise tenths and hundredths and remind the children that 6.2 is the same as 6.20 and thus is larger than 6.19. It is common for children to see 6.19 as larger than 6.2 due to a misunderstanding of the size of tenths and hundredths and the place value system.

100% New Developing Mathematics
Counting and Understanding
Number: Ages 10–11
© A & C BLACK

Weighty questions

- **This table shows the weight of some animals.**

kilograms	animals
less than 2	budgie
$2 \leq k < 4$	cat
$4 \leq k < 6$	hare
$6 \leq k < 8$	raccoon
$8 \leq k < 10$	dog

The numbers below show the weights of different animals.

- **Put them in order of size, smallest first.**

1

3·55	2·421
2·421	2·425
2·425	
3·4	
3	
2·5	
3·099	

2

4·074	
3·725	
2·8	
4·462	
3·98	
3·0	
2·789	

3

7·695	
7·975	
7·765	
7·9	
7·0	
7·567	
7·65	

4

8·531	
8·5	
8·135	
8·51	
8·315	
8·3	
8·513	

NOW TRY THIS!

- **On paper, sort all the decimals into the five groups shown in the table.**

Teachers' note At the start of the lesson discuss the 'less than' and 'less than or equal to' signs and the notation $2 \leq k < 4$ where k stands for the number of kilograms. Explain that this means numbers that lie between 2 and 4, including the number 2 itself.

100% New Developing Mathematics
Counting and Understanding
Number: Ages 10–11
© A & C BLACK

Coconut shy

• **Write the correct decimals on the coconuts.**

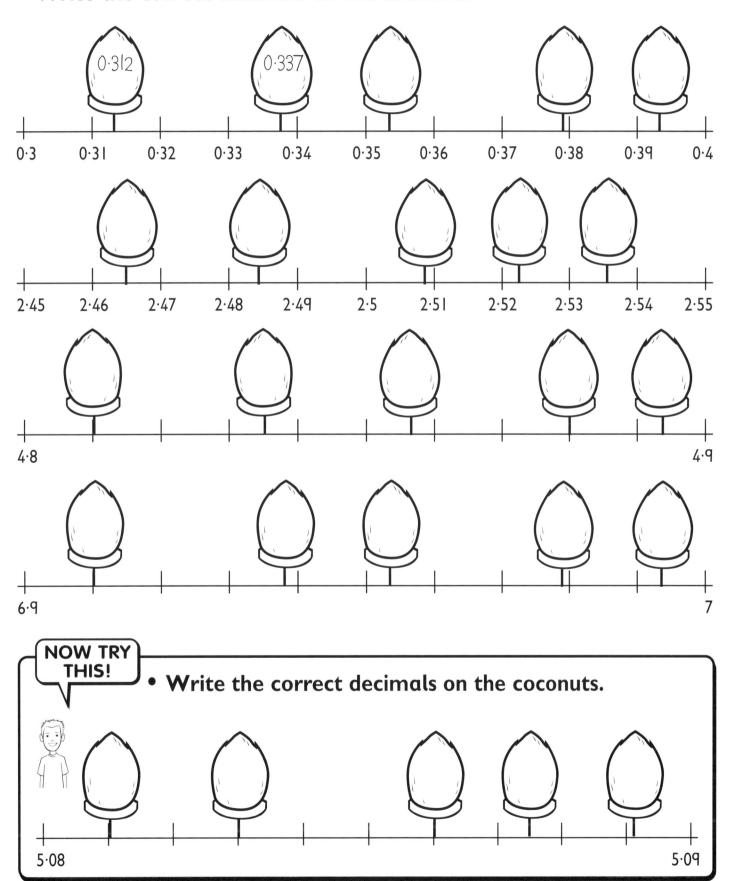

Number line 1: 0·3 ... 0·312 ... 0·32 ... 0·337 ... 0·34 ... 0·35 ... 0·36 ... 0·37 ... 0·38 ... 0·39 ... 0·4

Number line 2: 2·45 ... 2·46 ... 2·47 ... 2·48 ... 2·49 ... 2·5 ... 2·51 ... 2·52 ... 2·53 ... 2·54 ... 2·55

Number line 3: 4·8 ... 4·9

Number line 4: 6·9 ... 7

NOW TRY THIS!

• **Write the correct decimals on the coconuts.**

5·08 ... 5·09

Teachers' note Some children will find it easier to write all the decimals of the marked points under the line for the third, fourth and fifth number lines. Point out that the decimals marked on the line in the extension activity are in hundredths, rather than tenths.

100% New Developing Mathematics
Counting and Understanding
Number: Ages 10–11
© A & C BLACK

31

Decimal puzzle: 1

- **Cut out the small hexagons and arrange them onto the large hexagons to show each decimal on the large hexagon rounded to the nearest whole number.**

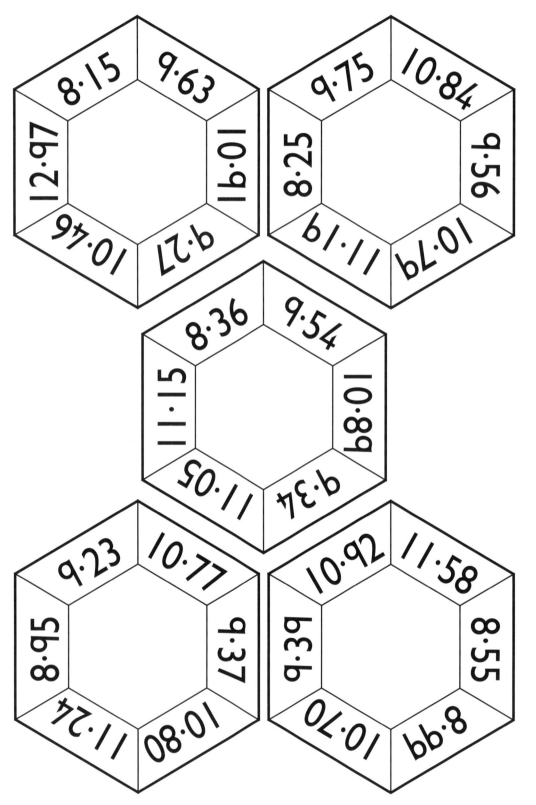

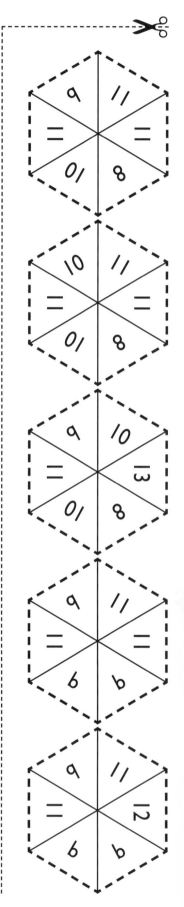

Teachers' note Ensure the children understand that there is only one correct position that each small hexagon can be placed where all the decimals are correctly rounded to the nearest whole number. Remind them that the digit 5 is rounded up, for example 4·5 is rounded to 5 and 3·53 is rounded to 4.

100% New Developing Mathematics
Counting and Understanding
Number: Ages 10–11
© A & C BLACK

Decimal puzzle: 2

- **Cut out the small hexagons and arrange them onto the large hexagons to show each decimal on the large hexagon rounded to the nearest tenth.**

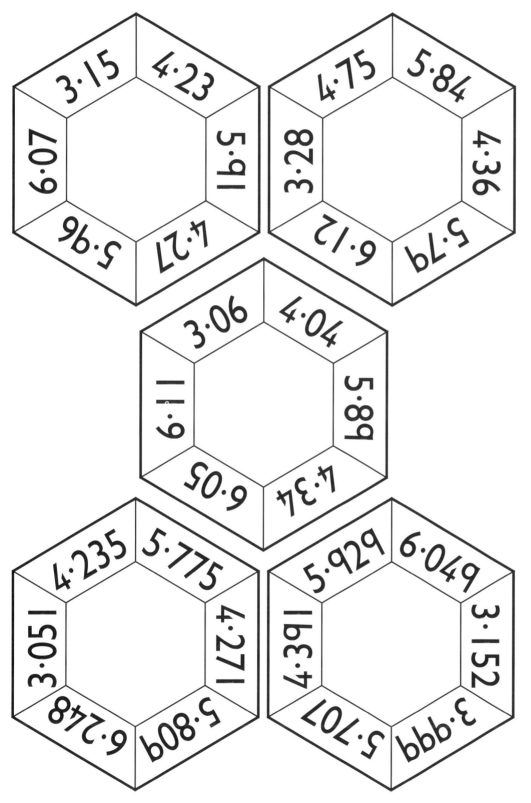

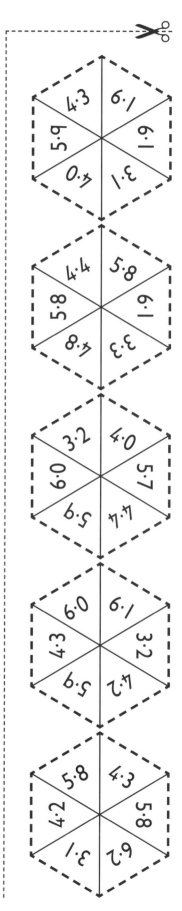

Teachers' note Ensure the children understand that there is only one correct position that each small hexagon can be placed where all the decimals are correctly rounded to the nearest tenth. Remind them that the digit 5 is rounded up, for example 4·35 is rounded to 4·4 and 2·953 is rounded to 3·0.

**100% New Developing Mathematics
Counting and Understanding
Number: Ages 10–11**
© A & C BLACK

Decimal puzzle: 3

- Cut out the small hexagons and arrange them onto the large hexagons to show each decimal on the large hexagon rounded to the nearest hundredth.

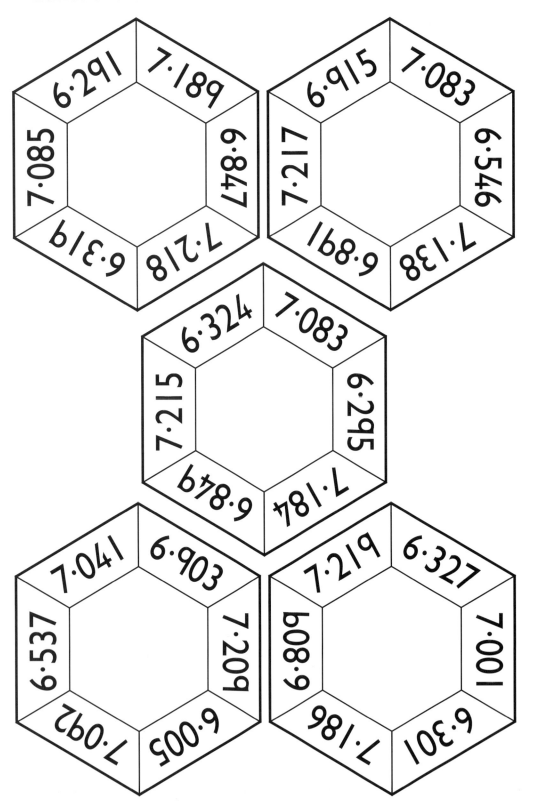

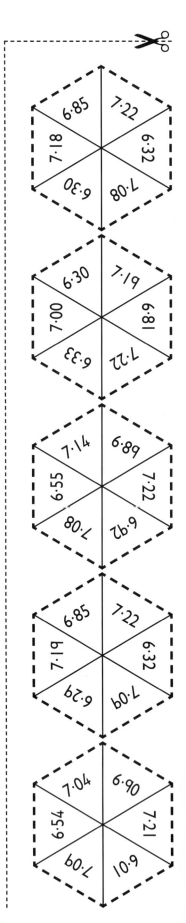

Teachers' note Ensure the children understand that there is only one correct position that each small hexagon can be placed where all the decimals are correctly rounded to the nearest hundredth. Remind them that the digit 5 is rounded up, for example 4·385 is rounded to 4·39 and 2·395 is rounded to 2·40 (to the nearest hundredth).

34

100% New Developing Mathematics
Counting and Understanding
Number: Ages 10–11
© A & C BLACK

Pack it in

- **Using the information in the box, give your answer as an improper fraction and as a mixed number.**

6 pots of yoghurt in one pack.

4 tins of beans in one pack.

5 bagels in one bag.

10 chunks of chocolate in one bar.

8 equal slices in one pizza.

- **What fraction of:**

1 a pack of yogurt is 7 pots?

$\dfrac{7}{6}$ $1\dfrac{1}{6}$

2 a chocolate bar is 13 chunks?

3 a pack of beans is 9 tins?

4 a pizza is 13 slices?

5 a bag of bagels is 14 bagels?

6 a pack of yogurt is 17 pots?

7 a chocolate bar is 27 chunks?

8 a pack of beans is 13 tins?

NOW TRY THIS!

- **Write these fractions as mixed numbers in their simplest form.**

$\dfrac{38}{6}$ $\dfrac{38}{4}$ $\dfrac{38}{5}$ $\dfrac{38}{10}$

Teachers' note It is important that children realise that each of the different wholes in the box have been split into a different number of equal parts. Thus when they decide what fraction of the whole is being described they must refer to the box to decide what the denominator of the improper fraction and mixed number will be.

**100% New Developing Mathematics
Counting and Understanding
Number: Ages 10–11
© A & C BLACK**

How are we related?

These two children are describing their shirt number in relation to the other's shirt number.

My number is $\frac{9}{10}$ of your number.

My number is $1\frac{1}{9}$ times your number.

- **Fill in the missing fractions or mixed numbers in these statements.**

1

My number is ____ of your number.

My number is ____ times your number.

2

My number is ____ of your number.

My number is ____ times your number.

3

My number is ____ of your number.

My number is ____ times your number.

4

My number is ____ of your number.

My number is ____ times your number.

5

My number is ____ of your number.

My number is ____ times your number.

NOW TRY THIS!

- **With a partner, choose a number each and write two statements about them in relation to each other.**

Teachers' note When finding the mixed number, children might find it easier to first write an improper fraction and then to convert it to a mixed number i.e. for the example at the top of the page the improper fraction $\frac{10}{9}$ is then converted to $1\frac{1}{9}$.

100% New Developing Mathematics Counting and Understanding Number: Ages 10–11 © A & C BLACK

Fraction quiz

In this quiz, a point is scored for each correct answer.
- **Tick the correct answers. There may be more than one each time.**
- **Work out Millie's, Billy's and Lily's scores at the end.**

		M	**B**	**L**
1	How many weeks is 15 days?	$2\frac{2}{7}$	$1\frac{1}{15}$	$2\frac{1}{7}$
2	How many weeks is 30 days?	$3\frac{2}{7}$	$4\frac{1}{2}$	$4\frac{2}{7}$
3	How many dozen is 41 eggs?	$3\frac{5}{12}$	$3\frac{1}{2}$	$3\frac{7}{12}$
4	How many years is 18 months?	$1\frac{6}{12}$	$1\frac{1}{2}$	$2\frac{1}{4}$
5	How many dozen is 54 eggs?	$4\frac{6}{12}$	$4\frac{1}{12}$	$4\frac{1}{2}$
6	How many days is 60 hours?	$2\frac{3}{4}$	$2\frac{12}{24}$	$2\frac{1}{2}$
7	How many years is 26 months?	$3\frac{3}{12}$	$2\frac{1}{12}$	$2\frac{1}{6}$
8	How many weeks is 47 days?	$6\frac{5}{7}$	$6\frac{4}{7}$	$5\frac{5}{7}$
9	How many dozen is 50 eggs?	$4\frac{1}{6}$	$4\frac{1}{2}$	$4\frac{2}{12}$
10	How many days is 36 hours?	$3\frac{1}{12}$	$1\frac{12}{24}$	$1\frac{1}{2}$

Scores _____   _____   _____

NOW TRY THIS!

- **Complete these statements with mixed numbers.**

  29 days is _____ weeks   29 eggs is _____ dozen

Teachers' note At the start of the lesson revise how many of each smaller unit are in the larger unit, listing them on the board, i.e. 1 week = 7 days, 1 dozen = 12 eggs, 12 months = 1 year, 1 day = 24 hours. Emphasise that the answers should be mixed numbers and may also be in their simplest form.

100% New Developing Mathematics
Counting and Understanding
Number: Ages 10–11
© A & C BLACK

A sure measure

- **For each question, write the fraction as an** | improper fraction | **and as a** | mixed number | **in its simplest form.**

1 What fraction of **1 metre** is each length?

a 150 cm $\dfrac{150}{100} = \dfrac{3}{2} = 1\dfrac{1}{2}$

b 225 cm _____

c 275 cm _____

d 310 cm _____

e 120 cm _____

f 290 cm _____

g 101 cm _____

h 135 cm _____

i 340 cm _____

j 260 cm _____

2 What fraction of **1 kilogram** is each weight?

a 1500 g $\dfrac{1500}{1000} = \dfrac{3}{2} = 1\dfrac{1}{2}$

b 2100 g _____

c 1001 g _____

d 1250 g _____

e 3750 g _____

f 2005 g _____

g 3200 g _____

h 1050 g _____

i 2350 g _____

j 4600 g _____

NOW TRY THIS!

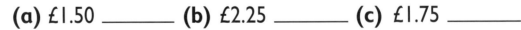

- **What fraction of** | £1 | **is each of these?**

(a) £1.50 _____   **(b)** £2.25 _____   **(c)** £1.75 _____

(d) £3.10 _____   **(e)** £7.50 _____   **(f)** £4.20 _____

Teachers' note An alternative way to tackle this page is for the children to write the amount as a decimal (essentially converting the measurement to metres or kilograms). They could then convert the decimal to a mixed number, and then an improper fraction.

**100% New Developing Mathematics
Counting and Understanding
Number: Ages 10–11**
© A & C BLACK

Domino loop

- **Cut along the dotted lines and make a domino loop.**

Play this game with a partner.

$19\frac{1}{2}$	$\frac{14}{3}$	$7\frac{6}{7}$	$\frac{9}{4}$	$2\frac{1}{4}$	$\frac{15}{4}$
$3\frac{3}{4}$	$\frac{13}{8}$	$5\frac{4}{5}$	$\frac{55}{9}$	$4\frac{2}{3}$	$\frac{55}{7}$
$6\frac{1}{9}$	$\frac{30}{7}$	$6\frac{1}{8}$	$\frac{23}{3}$	$1\frac{5}{8}$	$\frac{22}{3}$
$8\frac{1}{2}$	$\frac{34}{5}$	$6\frac{1}{7}$	$\frac{39}{2}$	$7\frac{1}{3}$	$\frac{11}{4}$
$5\frac{1}{3}$	$\frac{39}{4}$	$2\frac{3}{4}$	$\frac{16}{3}$	$6\frac{4}{5}$	$\frac{43}{7}$
$9\frac{3}{4}$	$\frac{50}{9}$	$8\frac{3}{4}$	$\frac{29}{9}$	$2\frac{2}{5}$	$\frac{19}{4}$
$4\frac{2}{7}$	$\frac{49}{8}$	$3\frac{2}{9}$	$\frac{29}{5}$	$7\frac{2}{3}$	$\frac{19}{10}$
$1\frac{9}{10}$	$\frac{17}{2}$	$5\frac{5}{9}$	$\frac{12}{5}$	$4\frac{3}{4}$	$\frac{35}{4}$

Teachers' note When making a loop, the children should convert the mixed number to an improper fraction and place the correct answer to lines left of it, or convert the improper fraction to a mixed number and place a domino showing this to the right of it. The children could time how quickly they complete the loop and then repeat, trying to improve their times.

**100% New Developing Mathematics
Counting and Understanding
Number: Ages 10–11**
© A & C BLACK

Robot twins

- **Write each fraction in its simplest form.**

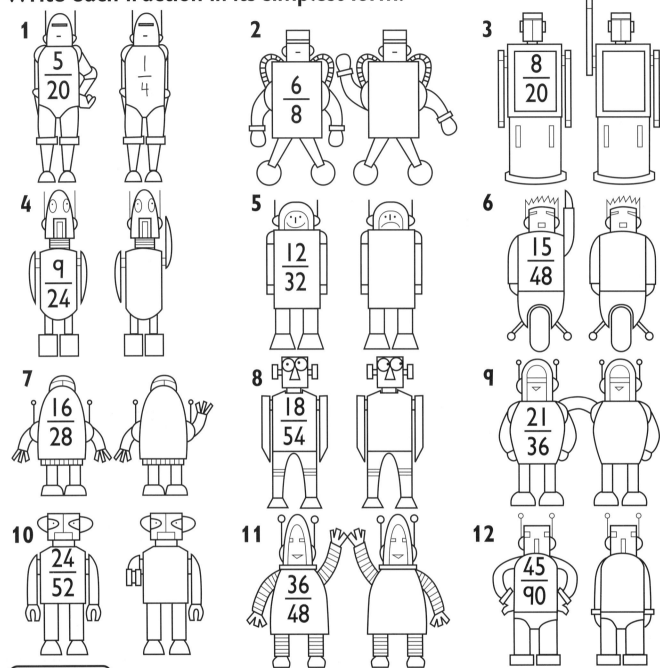

1 $\dfrac{5}{20}$ $\dfrac{1}{4}$

2 $\dfrac{6}{8}$

3 $\dfrac{8}{20}$

4 $\dfrac{9}{24}$

5 $\dfrac{12}{32}$

6 $\dfrac{15}{48}$

7 $\dfrac{16}{28}$

8 $\dfrac{18}{54}$

9 $\dfrac{21}{36}$

10 $\dfrac{24}{52}$

11 $\dfrac{36}{48}$

12 $\dfrac{45}{90}$

NOW TRY THIS!

- **Use these numbers to make ten different fractions.**
- **Write each fraction in its simplest form.**

12	8	48	400	24
100	50	36	56	300
500	16	20	64	88
32	200	80	72	320

Teachers' note Remind the children that when simplifying fractions, the numerator and the denominator should be divided by the largest number possible, leaving no remainders.

**100% New Developing Mathematics
Counting and Understanding
Number: Ages 10–11
© A & C BLACK**

I scream for ice-cream

• **Write each fraction in its simplest form.**

1 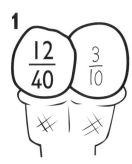 $\frac{12}{40}$ $\frac{3}{10}$

2 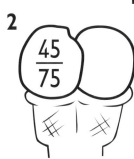 $\frac{45}{75}$

3 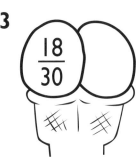 $\frac{18}{30}$

4  $\frac{45}{135}$

5 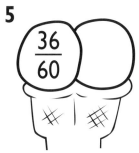 $\frac{36}{60}$

6  $\frac{24}{56}$

7 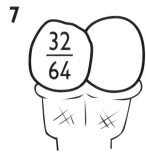 $\frac{32}{64}$

8  $\frac{28}{84}$

9 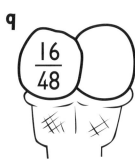 $\frac{16}{48}$

10 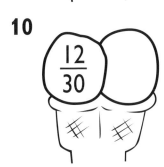 $\frac{12}{30}$

11  $\frac{24}{90}$

12  $\frac{17}{51}$

13 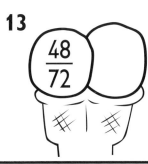 $\frac{48}{72}$

14 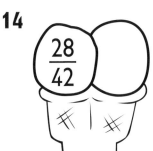 $\frac{28}{42}$

15 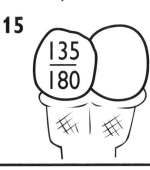 $\frac{135}{180}$

NOW TRY THIS!

• **What fraction of 40 is each number?**
  Give your answer in its simplest form.

10 $\frac{1}{4}$ 4 —   8 —   2 —   5 —   1 —

15 —   16 —   12 —   18 —   25 —   38 —

Teachers' note Remind the children that when simplifying fractions, the numerator and the denominator should be divided by the largest number possible, leaving no remainders.

100% New Developing Mathematics
Counting and Understanding
Number: Ages 10–11
© A & C BLACK

41

Colour by fractions

- Simplify the fractions in the picture to their simplest form and use the key to colour the picture.

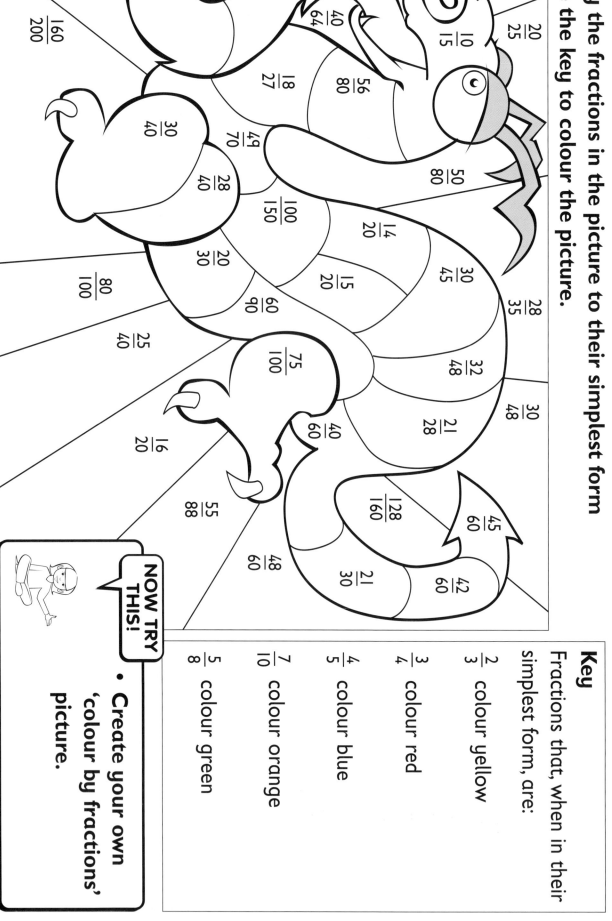

The fractions shown in the picture:

$\frac{8}{10}$ $\frac{20}{25}$ $\frac{10}{15}$ $\frac{40}{64}$ $\frac{40}{64}$ $\frac{250}{400}$ $\frac{14}{21}$ $\frac{35}{50}$ $\frac{160}{200}$ $\frac{18}{27}$ $\frac{56}{80}$ $\frac{50}{80}$ $\frac{30}{40}$ $\frac{49}{70}$ $\frac{28}{40}$ $\frac{100}{150}$ $\frac{14}{20}$ $\frac{30}{45}$ $\frac{28}{35}$ $\frac{20}{30}$ $\frac{15}{20}$ $\frac{32}{48}$ $\frac{80}{100}$ $\frac{60}{90}$ $\frac{30}{48}$ $\frac{25}{40}$ $\frac{75}{100}$ $\frac{21}{28}$ $\frac{16}{20}$ $\frac{40}{60}$ $\frac{55}{88}$ $\frac{128}{160}$ $\frac{45}{60}$ $\frac{48}{60}$ $\frac{21}{30}$ $\frac{42}{60}$

Key
Fractions that, when in their simplest form, are:

$\frac{2}{3}$ colour yellow

$\frac{3}{4}$ colour red

$\frac{4}{5}$ colour blue

$\frac{7}{10}$ colour orange

$\frac{5}{8}$ colour green

NOW TRY THIS!

- Create your own 'colour by fractions' picture.

100% New Developing Mathematics
Counting and Understanding
Number: Ages 10–11
© A & C BLACK

Teachers' note The children will need coloured pencils for this activity. Remind the children that when simplifying fractions, the numerator and the denominator should be divided by the largest number possible, leaving no remainders. This worksheet would form a useful homework activity, thus preventing the colours being copied from another child's worksheet.

Fraction line-up

- **Change each fraction so that it has the** common denominator **shown on the number line. Join the fraction to the line.**

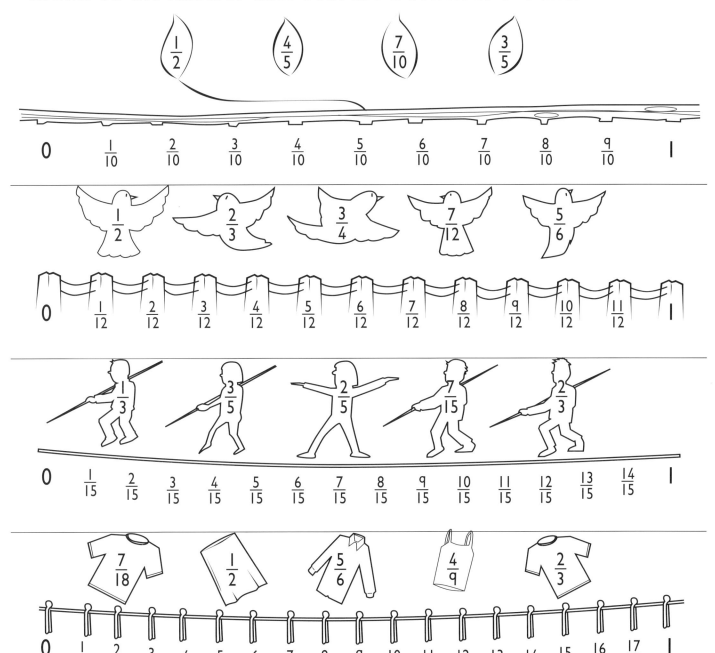

Teachers' note Point out to the children that not every fraction will need to be changed to an equivalent one as some will already have the new denominator.

100% New Developing Mathematics
Counting and Understanding
Number: Ages 10–11
© A & C BLACK

43

Fraction friends

- Convert each fraction to an equivalent one so that all three fractions have a common denominator.
- Then put the three fractions in order by writing **A**, **B** and **C** on the T-shirts (**A** is the smallest, **B** is the largest).

1 $\frac{2}{3}$ B $\frac{20}{30}$ $\frac{3}{5}$ A $\frac{18}{30}$ $\frac{7}{10}$ C $\frac{21}{30}$

2 $\frac{3}{5}$ $\frac{7}{10}$ $\frac{1}{2}$

3 $\frac{5}{6}$ $\frac{7}{9}$ $\frac{2}{3}$

4 $\frac{1}{4}$ $\frac{5}{12}$ $\frac{3}{8}$

5 $\frac{4}{7}$ $\frac{9}{14}$ $\frac{2}{3}$

6 $\frac{7}{8}$ $\frac{4}{5}$ $\frac{9}{10}$

NOW TRY THIS!
- Write five fractions with different denominators.
- Order the fractions using the letters **A, B, C, D** and **E**.

44

Teachers' note At the start of the lesson, demonstrate how to choose a common denominator. Show the children how to look at the denominators in the set to find a number that each divides into without leaving a remainder. Then show how the numerator and the denominator of a fraction must be multiplied by the same number to create an equivalent fraction.

100% New Developing Mathematics
Counting and Understanding
Number: Ages 10–11
© A & C BLACK

Fraction spell

- **Change each fraction to an equivalent one so that all five fractions have a common denominator.**
- **Order the fractions, smallest to largest, to spell a word.**

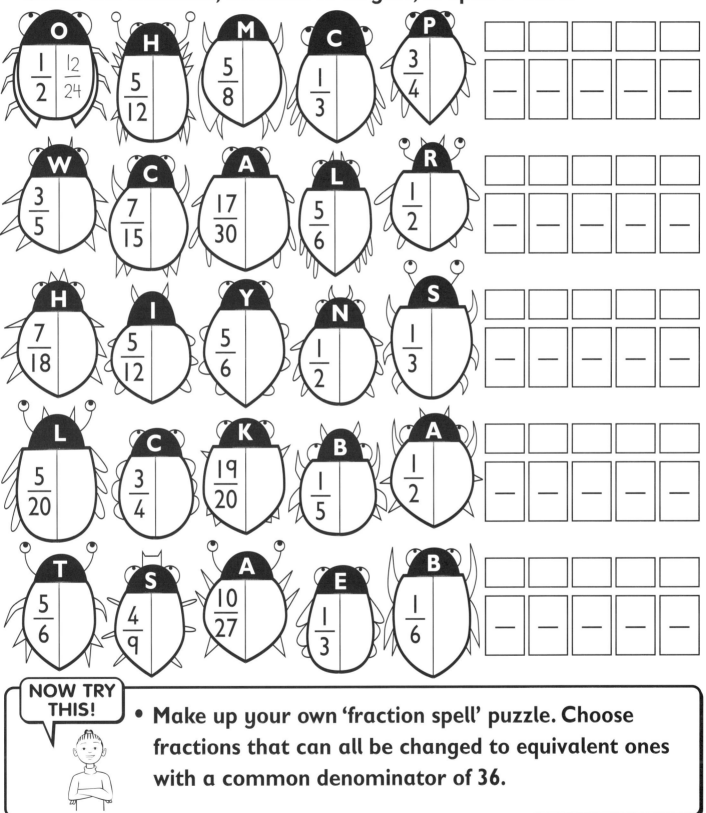

O $\dfrac{1}{2}$ $\dfrac{12}{24}$ H $\dfrac{5}{12}$ M $\dfrac{5}{8}$ C $\dfrac{1}{3}$ P $\dfrac{3}{4}$

W $\dfrac{3}{5}$ C $\dfrac{7}{15}$ A $\dfrac{17}{30}$ L $\dfrac{5}{6}$ R $\dfrac{1}{2}$

H $\dfrac{7}{18}$ I $\dfrac{5}{12}$ Y $\dfrac{5}{6}$ N $\dfrac{1}{2}$ S $\dfrac{1}{3}$

L $\dfrac{5}{20}$ C $\dfrac{3}{4}$ K $\dfrac{19}{20}$ B $\dfrac{1}{5}$ A $\dfrac{1}{2}$

T $\dfrac{5}{6}$ S $\dfrac{4}{9}$ A $\dfrac{10}{27}$ E $\dfrac{1}{3}$ B $\dfrac{1}{6}$

NOW TRY THIS!

- **Make up your own 'fraction spell' puzzle. Choose fractions that can all be changed to equivalent ones with a common denominator of 36.**

Teachers' note When the children are making up their own puzzles, encourage them to begin with a five-letter word, for example SPEAR or HOUSE, and then to allocate a fraction for each letter, in order. They should then copy out the fractions, with their corresponding letters, in a jumbled order for their partner to solve. These puzzles can form a stimulating classroom display.

**100% New Developing Mathematics
Counting and Understanding
Number: Ages 10–11
© A & C BLACK**

Telly addict

This TV guide shows the lengths of some programmes, written in fractions of an hour.

- **How long will each programme be in minutes?**

Convert each fraction to an equivalent one with a denominator of 60 to help you.

The Strongest Link	$\frac{3}{4}$ of an hour	_45_ mins
Enemies	$\frac{1}{2}$ an hour	_____ mins
Cartoon Mania	$\frac{3}{20}$ of an hour	_____ mins
The News	$\frac{7}{10}$ of an hour	_____ mins
Film Focus	$\frac{11}{15}$ of an hour	_____ mins
Bart's Art	$\frac{1}{3}$ of an hour	_____ mins
Kool Kids	$\frac{13}{30}$ of an hour	_____ mins
Cops	$\frac{3}{60}$ of an hour	_____ mins
The Stimpsons	$\frac{1}{6}$ of an hour	_____ mins
Jungle People	$\frac{1}{4}$ of an hour	_____ mins
Westenders	$\frac{2}{5}$ of an hour	_____ mins
Indignation Street	$\frac{3}{10}$ of an hour	_____ mins
Gemmadale	$\frac{2}{3}$ of an hour	_____ mins

- **Write each fraction in order. Start with the shortest programme.**

NOW TRY THIS!

- **Put these fractions of a day in order, starting with the smallest.**

$\frac{3}{4}$ $\frac{1}{6}$ $\frac{5}{8}$ $\frac{11}{12}$ $\frac{2}{3}$ $\frac{1}{2}$ $\frac{7}{24}$ $\frac{5}{6}$

Convert each fraction to an equivalent one with a denominator of 24 to help you.

Teachers' note Remind the children that, when finding equivalent fractions, both the numerator and the denominator must be multiplied or divided by the same number. Here, children should look at the existing denominator and decide what it must be multiplied by to make 60. They should then multiply the numerator by that number.

100% New Developing Mathematics
Counting and Understanding
Number: Ages 10–11
© A & C BLACK

Top that!: 1

- ## Cut out the cards and play 'Top that!' with a partner.

Greece

Population	10 690 000
Male	49·1%
Female	50·9%
Aged 0–14 years	14·3%
Aged 15–64 years	66·7%
Aged 65+	19·0%

UK

Population	60 610 000
Male	49·5%
Female	50·5%
Aged 0–14 years	17·5%
Aged 15–64 years	66·8%
Aged 65+	15·7%

Australia

Population	20 260 000
Male	49·7%
Female	50·3%
Aged 0–14 years	19·6%
Aged 15–64 years	67·3%
Aged 65+	13·1%

China

Population	1 313 970 000
Male	51·5%
Female	48·5%
Aged 0–14 years	20·8%
Aged 15–64 years	71·5%
Aged 65+	7·7%

Ethiopia

Population	74 780 000
Male	49·9%
Female	50·1%
Aged 0–14 years	43·7%
Aged 15–64 years	53·6%
Aged 65+	2·7%

Japan

Population	127 460 000
Male	48·8%
Female	51·2%
Aged 0–14 years	14·3%
Aged 15–64 years	65·7%
Aged 65+	20·0%

USA

Population	298 440 000
Male	49·1%
Female	50·9%
Aged 0–14 years	20·4%
Aged 15–64 years	67·2%
Aged 65+	12·4%

Kazakhstan

Population	15 230 000
Male	48·3%
Female	51·7%
Aged 0–14 years	23·0%
Aged 15–64 years	68·8%
Aged 65+	8·2%

Teachers' note Each child has a pile of eight cards. Both players turn a card. Player 1 chooses a category s/he thinks most likely to win, for example percentage of people aged 65+, and both players say the percentage on their card. The player with the highest percentage wins the cards. Players pick a new card and player 2 chooses the category. The player with the most cards at the end wins.

**100% New Developing Mathematics
Counting and Understanding
Number: Ages 10–11**
© A & C BLACK

Top that!: 2

- **Cut out the cards and play 'Top that!' with a partner.**

France

Population	60 880 000
Male	48·8%
Female	51·2%
Aged 0–14 years	18·3%
Aged 15–64 years	65·3%
Aged 65+	16·4%

India

Population	1 095 350 000
Male	51·5%
Female	48·5%
Aged 0–14 years	30·8%
Aged 15–64 years	64·3%
Aged 65+	4·9%

Bolivia

Population	8 990 000
Male	49·5%
Female	50·5%
Aged 0–14 years	35·0%
Aged 15–64 years	60·4%
Aged 65+	4·6%

Russia

Population	142 890 000
Male	46·4%
Female	53·6%
Aged 0–14 years	14·2%
Aged 15–64 years	71·4%
Aged 65+	14·4%

Iceland

Population	300 000
Male	50·0%
Female	50·0%
Aged 0–14 years	21·7%
Aged 15–64 years	66·6%
Aged 65+	11·7%

Morocco

Population	33 240 000
Male	49·9%
Female	50·1%
Aged 0–14 years	31·6%
Aged 15–64 years	63·4%
Aged 65+	5·0%

Albania

Population	3 580 000
Male	51·0%
Female	49·0%
Aged 0–14 years	24·8%
Aged 15–64 years	66·3%
Aged 65+	8·9%

Mexico

Population	107 450 000
Male	49·0%
Female	51·0%
Aged 0–14 years	30·6%
Aged 15–64 years	63·6%
Aged 65+	5·8%

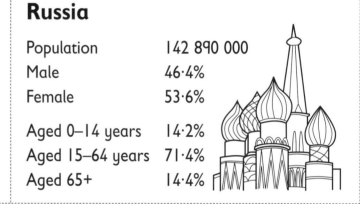

Teachers' note This sheet should be used in conjunction with page 47.

100% New Developing Mathematics
Counting and Understanding
Number: Ages 10–11
© A & C BLACK

Percentage code

- **Convert each fraction to an equivalent one with a denominator of 100 and write it as an equivalent percentage.**
- **Use the key to spell out the name of a fraction.**

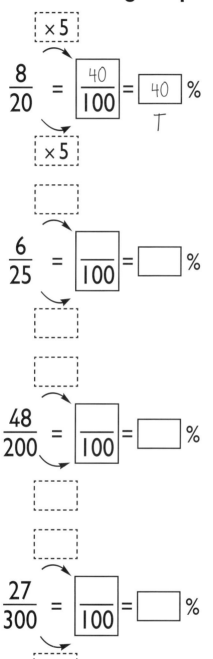

$[\times 5]$

$\dfrac{8}{20} = \dfrac{40}{100} = \boxed{40}\ \%$
  T

$[\times 5]$

$\dfrac{6}{25} = \dfrac{}{100} = \boxed{}\ \%$

$\dfrac{48}{200} = \dfrac{}{100} = \boxed{}\ \%$

$\dfrac{27}{300} = \dfrac{}{100} = \boxed{}\ \%$

$\dfrac{5}{25} = \dfrac{}{100} = \boxed{}\ \%$

$\dfrac{7}{10} = \dfrac{}{100} = \boxed{}\ \%$

$\dfrac{3}{4} = \dfrac{}{100} = \boxed{}\ \%$

$\dfrac{36}{50} = \dfrac{}{100} = \boxed{}\ \%$

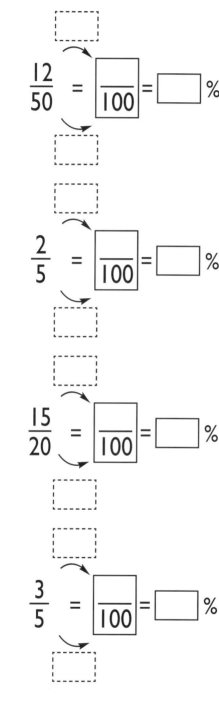

$\dfrac{12}{50} = \dfrac{}{100} = \boxed{}\ \%$

$\dfrac{2}{5} = \dfrac{}{100} = \boxed{}\ \%$

$\dfrac{15}{20} = \dfrac{}{100} = \boxed{}\ \%$

$\dfrac{3}{5} = \dfrac{}{100} = \boxed{}\ \%$

Key

A	35%	E	60%	I	9%	O	24%	U	70%	F	75%
S	22%	T	40%	V	72%	W	20%	L	55%	R	30%

Teachers' note Point out to the children that sometimes they will have to multiply and sometimes divide in order to convert the fractions. Provide the children with a calculator to check their answers and show them that fractions can be converted to percentages by dividing the numerator by the denominator and then multiplying by 100.

100% New Developing Mathematics
Counting and Understanding
Number: Ages 10–11
© A & C BLACK

gBay

On an online shopping site, people selling items (sellers) are scored positively or negatively.

Their 'rating' is the number of positive scores out of the total number of scores, given as a percentage.

• **Work out the percentages for each seller.**

gbay

categories

search

shop

my gbay

cart

help

◀ ▶

Seller	Positive scores	Total scores	Percentage rating
'loads2sell'	42	50	84%
'moneybags'	8	10	
'sellagain'	21	25	
'buynow'	19	20	
'Davesdeals'	43	50	
'TVs4u'	4	5	
'superseller!'	3	4	
'robme'	18	20	
'best1'	24	25	
'me2u'	180	200	
'The12C'	420	500	
'££cash££'	870	1000	
'dodgydan'	90	300	
'gr8deals'	4500	5000	
'buyfromme'	360	400	
'powerseller'	9100	10 000	

NOW TRY THIS!

• **Write five sets of scores that would have a rating of 85%.**

Teachers' note Encourage the children to think of each score as a fraction first, and then to convert the fraction so that it has a denominator of 100 in order to convert it to a percentage. As a check, provide the children with a calculator and show them that fractions can be converted to percentages by dividing the numerator by the denominator and then multiplying by 100.

100% New Developing Mathematics
Counting and Understanding
Number: Ages 10–11
© A & C BLACK

Cat and mouse

• **Play this game with a partner.**

☆ Decide who is the cat and who is the mouse. Then place your counters on the starting positions.

☆ The mouse goes first, moving one space in any direction to a touching square. It can then jump to any space that shows an equivalent amount to the square it has landed on.

☆ The cat moves next, in the same way. The aim for the cat is to jump on the mouse. The aim for the mouse is to escape the cat!

☆ If the mouse survives for 20 moves, it wins. If not, the cat wins.

You need a different coloured counter each.

$\dfrac{1}{3}$	$\dfrac{1}{10}$	40%	0·6	$\dfrac{3}{4}$	**start**
$\dfrac{1}{5}$	7%	$\dfrac{53}{100}$	$\dfrac{1}{2}$	20%	0·4
0·5	0·333	0·75	0·53	0·07	0·9
14%	$\dfrac{3}{5}$	25%	10%	0·666	33·3%
$\dfrac{7}{50}$	$\dfrac{2}{5}$	50%	**start**	$\dfrac{1}{4}$	$\dfrac{2}{3}$
0·2	0·1	$\dfrac{7}{100}$	0·25	0·07	0·14
60%	66·6%	$\dfrac{9}{10}$	90%	75%	53%

Teachers' note   Ensure that the children realise that 'any direction' means up or down, sideways or diagonally, Encourage the children to play the game several times, swapping roles. As an extension, invite the children to write all the fractions, decimals and percentages into a three-columned table, showing equivalents in the same row.

100% New Developing Mathematics
Counting and Understanding
Number: Ages 10–11
© A & C BLACK

Hoopla stall

- **Ring the fractions that are equivalent to each percentage.**

More than one fraction can be ringed.

40%	$\frac{2}{5}$	$\frac{8}{10}$	$\frac{40}{60}$	$\frac{40}{100}$	$\frac{5}{8}$	$\frac{4}{10}$
60%	$\frac{3}{5}$	$\frac{30}{50}$	$\frac{6}{10}$	$\frac{19}{3}$	$\frac{60}{100}$	$\frac{3}{6}$
75%	$\frac{18}{24}$	$\frac{3}{4}$	$\frac{12}{16}$	$\frac{9}{12}$	$\frac{6}{8}$	$\frac{8}{12}$
15%	$\frac{15}{30}$	$\frac{7}{50}$	$\frac{15}{100}$	$\frac{3}{50}$	$\frac{3}{20}$	$\frac{1}{15}$
90%	$\frac{9}{10}$	$\frac{90}{10}$	$\frac{18}{20}$	$\frac{90}{100}$	$\frac{10}{9}$	$\frac{45}{50}$
25%	$\frac{1}{4}$	$\frac{5}{20}$	$\frac{15}{60}$	$\frac{8}{32}$	$\frac{25}{100}$	$\frac{4}{24}$
35%	$\frac{7}{20}$	$\frac{35}{10}$	$\frac{35}{100}$	$\frac{100}{35}$	$\frac{3}{5}$	$\frac{35}{50}$
64%	$\frac{32}{50}$	$\frac{64}{10}$	$\frac{128}{200}$	$\frac{16}{25}$	$\frac{64}{100}$	$\frac{8}{13}$

NOW TRY THIS!

- **Write six different fractions that are equivalent to 80%.**

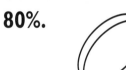   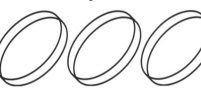

Teachers' note This type of question occurs in National Test papers and involves children (a) understanding how percentages can be converted into fractions, and (b) appreciating that there are many equivalent fractions for each percentage.

**100% New Developing Mathematics
Counting and Understanding
Number: Ages 10–11
© A & C BLACK**

Colour it!

- **Count the number of small shapes in each pattern.**
- **Colour the correct percentage of each shape.**

1

Colour 75% blue.

2

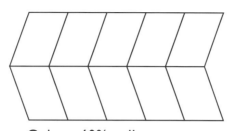

Colour 40% yellow and 10% red.

3

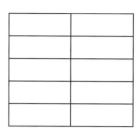

Colour 70% green and 20% blue.

4

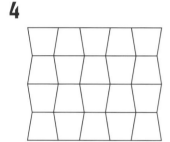

Colour 30% yellow, 15% red and 20% green.

5

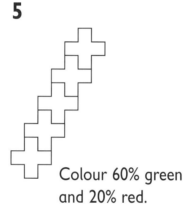

Colour 60% green and 20% red.

6

Colour 45% blue, 5% red and 35% yellow.

7

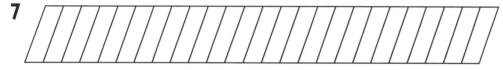

Colour 8% blue, 24% red and 40% yellow.

8

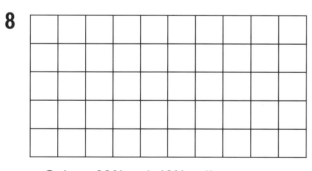

Colour 22% red, 48% yellow and 2% blue.

9

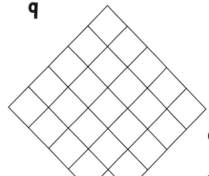

Colour 4% green, 16% yellow and 28% red.

NOW TRY THIS!

- **Calculate the percentage of each shape that is <u>not</u> coloured. Write this percentage next to the shape.**

Teachers' note Demonstrate how to (a) write each percentage as a fraction with a denominator of 100, and (b) convert the fraction to an equivalent one with a denominator that matches the number of small shapes in each pattern. For example in question 9, 4% is written as $\frac{4}{100}$, which converts to $\frac{1}{25}$.

**100% New Developing Mathematics
Counting and Understanding
Number: Ages 10–11
© A & C BLACK**

Dragon's labyrinth

- ## You need a coin for this activity.

☆ Keep tossing the coin to lead you through the labyrinth.

☆ As you go through, turn the fractions and decimals into percentages, and keep a running total.

☆ Stop when you reach a dagger.

☆ Do this many times. What is the **highest** total you can make?

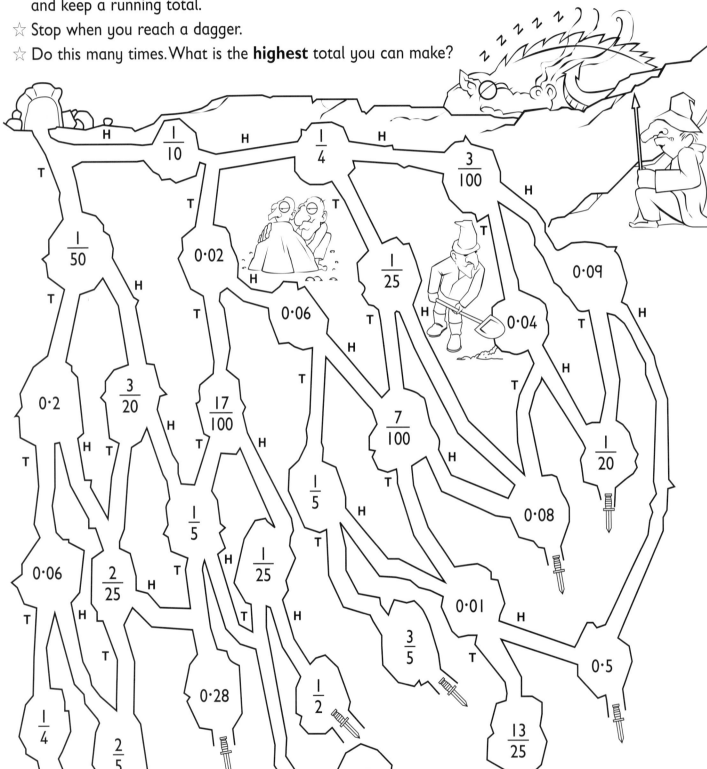

Teachers' note This activity can help children to see the usefulness of using percentages, as they are easier to compare and total than a mixture of fractions and decimals. Revise the equivalents at the start of the lesson and show the children how to convert fractions that they do not know into percentages, by converting to fractions with a denominator of 100.

**100% New Developing Mathematics
Counting and Understanding
Number: Ages 10–11**
© A & C BLACK

Virus alert!

A computer virus has deleted lots of the numbers on Kieran's work.

1 Fill in the missing numbers.

a The percentage **40%** of an amount means 4 tenths or _____ hundredths.

This is the fraction $\dfrac{}{100}$ or $\dfrac{}{10}$, which is equivalent to $\dfrac{}{5}$.

b The percentage **25%** means _____ hundredths.

This is the fraction $\dfrac{}{100}$, which in its simplest form is $\dfrac{}{}$.

c The percentage **5%** means _____ hundredths.

This is the fraction $\dfrac{}{100}$, which in its simplest form is $\dfrac{}{}$.

d The percentage **4%** means _____ hundredths.

This is the fraction $\dfrac{}{100}$, which in its simplest form is $\dfrac{}{}$.

e The percentage **60%** means _____ tenths or _____ hundredths.

This is the fraction $\dfrac{}{100}$ or $\dfrac{}{10}$, which in its simplest form is $\dfrac{}{}$.

f The percentage **68%** means _____ hundredths.

This is the fraction $\dfrac{}{100}$, which in its simplest form is $\dfrac{}{}$.

2 Now write the equivalent decimal for each percentage.

a _____   **b** _____   **c** _____   **d** _____   **e** _____   **f** _____

NOW TRY THIS!

- **Write six statements of your own like Kieran's.**

Teachers' note Demonstrate how to (a) write each percentage as a fraction with the denominator of 100, and (b) convert the fraction to equivalents, including the fraction in its simplest form.

100% New Developing Mathematics
Counting and Understanding
Number: Ages 10–11
© A & C BLACK

Clever conversions

This diagram shows how you can change fractions into decimals, and then into percentages.

It also shows how whole number percentages can be changed into fractions.

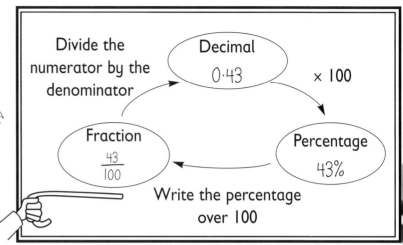

Divide the numerator by the denominator

Decimal
0·43

× 100

Fraction
$\frac{43}{100}$

Percentage
43%

Write the percentage over 100

• **Use the diagram and a calculator to help you fill in the tables.**

Fractions	Decimals	Percentages

Fractions	Decimals	Percentages

NOW TRY THIS!

• **Explore the fractions $\frac{1}{3}$, $\frac{2}{3}$, $\frac{1}{6}$ and $\frac{5}{6}$.**

**100% New Developing Mathematics
Counting and Understanding
Number: Ages 10–11**
© A & C BLACK

Hens and chicks

There are ⟦2⟧ chicks to ⟦7⟧ hens in the farmyard.

- **Use the diagram to help you answer the questions.**

1 How many chicks are in the yard if there are:

a   12 hens? _____

b   4 hens? _____

c   18 hens? _____

d   26 hens? _____

e   30 hens? _____

f   22 hens? _____

2 How many hens are in the yard if there are:

a   21 chicks? _____

b   35 chicks? _____

c   49 chicks? _____

d   28 chicks? _____

e   56 chicks? _____

f   84 chicks? _____

NOW TRY THIS!

- **How many hens and chicks are in the yard if there are:**

  a 36 birds?   **b** 54 birds?   **c** 108 birds?

  _____ hens   _____ hens   _____ hens

  _____ chicks   _____ chicks   _____ chicks

Teachers' note A ratio diagram helps children to understand scaling up or down in a given ratio. Demonstrate how the diagram can be used to find the given number of hens, chicks or birds. When this has been found, the corresponding number of hens or chicks can be identified.

100% New Developing Mathematics
Counting and Understanding
Number: Ages 10–11
© A & C BLACK

Spoon it out

One teaspoon holds 5 ml.　　One tablespoon holds 15 ml.

- **Cut out the cards and sort them into equivalent groups, three in each group.**
- **Fill in the blank cards to make more equivalents.**

3 tablespoons	**15 ml**	15 teaspoons	**30 ml**
6 teaspoons	2 tablespoons	**45 ml**	9 teaspoons
5 tablespoons	**60 ml**	12 teaspoons	**75 ml**
1 tablespoon	3 teaspoons	___ **ml**	4 tablespoons
___ **ml**	___ tablespoons	___ teaspoons	___ teaspoons
___ tablespoons	___ teaspoons	___ **ml**	___ tablespoons

Teachers' note Once the cards have been sorted and new equivalent groups have been completed, ask the children to remove the 'ml' cards. Without the help of the tablespoon cards, the children should shuffle the cards and try to match pairs of equivalents. Encourage them to look for multiplicative patterns in the numbers of teaspoons and millilitres.

100% New Developing Mathematics Counting and Understanding Number: Ages 10–11 © A & C BLACK

'Coven' Garden Market

☆ Cut out the cards.

☆ Pick a large card and a small card.

☆ Work out the calculation and record it on paper.

2 spider webs cost 60p 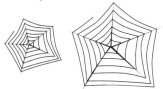	4 hairy moles cost 88p 	3 maggoty apples cost 90p 
5 phials of venom cost £10 	6 boxes of dandruff flakes cost £6.60 	2 snail shells cost £1.20 
5 toad warts cost £1.25 	3 owl pellets cost 93p 	6 jars of slug slime cost £18 
2 plugs of earwax cost £1.80 	4 pots of spots cost £5 	2 balls of bellybutton fluff cost £1.60 
4 bags of bat droppings cost £2.40 	3 tubs of toenail clippings cost £6.90 	5 bottles of cat spit cost £6 

Find the cost of one.	Find the cost of two.	Find the cost of three.	Find the cost of four.
Find the cost of five.	Find the cost of six.	Find the cost of seven.	Find the cost of eight.
Find the cost of nine.	Find the cost of ten.	Find the cost of eleven.	Find the cost of twelve.

Teachers' note Explain to the children that if they draw two cards with the same number of items, they should replace one of them and pick a new card. Encourage the children to work out how much one item costs first, before working out the new quantity.

100% New Developing Mathematics
Counting and Understanding
Number: Ages 10–11
© A & C BLACK

Great grams

Flour
Price per 100 g: 60p

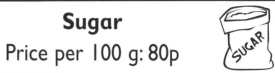
Sugar
Price per 100 g: 80p

Oats
Price per 100 g: £1.20

Butter
Price per 100 g: £1.10

- **Answer these proportion questions, using the information on the food labels.**

1 How much would Liam pay for:

a   300 g of flour? _____

b   200 g of sugar? _____

c   50 g of oats? _____

d   50 g of butter? _____

e   150 g of flour? _____

f   250 g of sugar? _____

g   450 g of oats? _____

h   350 g of butter? _____

i   750 g of flour? _____

j   950 g of sugar? _____

k   125 g of oats? _____

l   650 g of butter? _____

2 How many grams did Katie buy, if she spent:

a   £2.40 on flour? _____ g

b   £2.40 on sugar? _____ g

c   £2.40 on oats? _____ g

d   £3.30 on butter? _____ g

e   £1.50 on flour? _____ g

f   £2 on sugar? _____ g

g   £2.70 on oats? _____ g

h   £11 on butter? _____ g

i   75p on flour? _____ g

j   £1.40 on sugar? _____ g

k   £3.90 on oats? _____ g

l   £4.95 on butter? _____ g

NOW TRY THIS!

- **How much is each item** | per gram | **?**

flour _____ p   sugar _____ p   oats _____ p   butter _____ p

Teachers' note Encourage the children to describe their own methods for working out these proportions. Discuss effective methods and encourage the children to try each others' approaches. The prices can be masked and altered before the sheet is copied for further practice.

100% New Developing Mathemati
Counting and Understanding
Number: Ages 10–11
© A & C BLACK

Are we nearly there?

The Jones family travel from Town **A** to Town **C**,
a distance of 60 km. They stop on the way at Town **B**.

1 If the distance from A to B is **twice** as far as from B to C,
how far is the distance from A to B? _____ km

A   B   C

|←————————————————— 60 km ——————————————————→|

2 If the distance from A to B is **three times** as far as from B to C,
how far is the distance from A to B? _____ km

A   B   C

|←————————————————— 60 km ——————————————————→|

3 If the distance from A to B is **four times** as far as from B to C,
how far is the distance from A to B? _____ km

A   B   C

|←————————————————— 60 km ——————————————————→|

4 If the distance from A to B is **five times** as far as from B to C,
how far is the distance from A to B? _____ km

A   B   C

|←————————————————— 60 km ——————————————————→|

5 If the distance from A to B is **nine times** as far as from B to C,
how far is the distance from A to B? _____ km

A   B   C

|←————————————————— 60 km ——————————————————→|

NOW TRY THIS!

- **Imagine that the distance from A to C has changed.
  Answer each question above for these new distances.**
  a 180 km   **b** 90 km

Teachers' note This activity provides a useful context for some discussion about proportions. When the children have completed questions 1 to 5, ask them, in pairs, to discuss how they worked out each answer. This type of question can be given orally and the children asked to discuss their strategies for working out the answers.

**100% New Developing Mathematics
Counting and Understanding
Number: Ages 10–11
© A & C BLACK**

Cooking crisis

More people than expected have arrived at Jamie's restaurant.

• **Help him to rewrite his recipes.**

1

Creamy pea soup for 7 people

175 g butter

210 g peas

350 ml vegetable stock

98 ml double cream

7 tbsp chopped parsley

Creamy pea soup for **9 people**

_225_ g butter

_____ g peas

_____ ml vegetable stock

_____ ml double cream

_____ tbsp chopped parsley

2

Beef Baldaire for 3 people

3 garlic cloves

360 g chopped beef

60 ml tomato purée

6 chopped onions

420 g button mushrooms

270 g chopped tomatoes

Beef Baldaire for **8 people**

_____ garlic cloves

_____ g chopped beef

_____ ml tomato purée

_____ chopped onions

_____ g button mushrooms

_____ g chopped tomatoes

3

Marble cake for 4 people

240 g butter

280 g caster sugar

80 g ground almonds

140 g self-raising flour

4 eggs

148 g plain chocolate

Marble cake for **7 people**

_____ g butter

_____ g caster sugar

_____ g ground almonds

_____ g self-raising flour

_____ eggs

_____ g plain chocolate

NOW TRY THIS!

• **Now write how much of each ingredient would be needed to make each recipe for** `10` **people.**

Teachers' note At the start of the lesson, demonstrate how to divide each amount by the number of people stated at the top of the recipe to find how much for one person, and then multiply to find how much for several people.

100% New Developing Mathematic
Counting and Understanding
Number: Ages 10–11
© A & C BLACK

Answers

p 17

1 7	**2** 12	**3** 7	**4** 3	**5** 16
6 6	**7** 9	**8** 18	**9** 7	**10** 17
11 15	**12** 16	**13** 13	**14** 11	

p 18

1 a	30 °C	**b**	31 °C	**c**	29 °C	**d**	20 °C
2 a	15 °C	**b**	21 °C	**c**	34 °C	**d**	40 °C
3 a	14 °C	**b**	10 °C	**c**	35 °C	**d**	31 °C

Now try this!
Base Camp 55 °C

p 19

1 a	125 °C	**b**	180 °C	**c**	240 °C	**d**	340 °C
e	110 °C	**f**	0 °C	**g**	119 °C	**h**	398 °C
i	318 °C	**j**	277 °C						

| **2 a** Station 10 | **b** Station 4 |

| **3 a** | 25 °C | **b** | 20 °C | **c** | 34 °C | **d** | 74 °C |
| **e** | 2 °C | **f** | 44 °C | **g** | 7 °C | **h** | 88 °C |

Now try this!

Stations 1 and 5   Stations 1 and 4   Stations 2 and 6
Stations 4 and 5   Stations 4 and 8   Stations 4 and 10

p 24

| 8 1 | 2 8 | 3 9 | 0 5 |
| 4 0 | 0 5 | 0 8 | 9 7 |

Now try this!
5·205   0·055   25·255   0·505

p 28

8 + 0·6 + 0·04 + 0·031	8 + 0·4 + 0·27 + 0·001
8 + 0·6 + 0·03 + 0·041	8 + 0·3 + 0·37 + 0·001
8 + 0·6 + 0·02 + 0·051	8 + 0·2 + 0·47 + 0·001
	8 + 0·1 + 0·57 + 0·001

6 + 2·6 + 0·07 + 0·001	9 + 0·4 + 0·03 + 0·028
5 + 3·6 + 0·07 + 0·001	9 + 0·4 + 0·02 + 0·038
4 + 4·6 + 0·07 + 0·001	9 + 0·4 + 0·01 + 0·048
3 + 5·6 + 0·07 + 0·001	9 + 0·4 + 0·00 + 0·058

9 + 0·2 + 0·25 + 0·008	8 + 1·4 + 0·05 + 0·008
9 + 0·1 + 0·35 + 0·008	7 + 2·4 + 0·05 + 0·008
9 + 0·0 + 0·45 + 0·008	6 + 3·4 + 0·05 + 0·008
	5 + 4·4 + 0·05 + 0·008

p 29

0·183, 0·429, 0·47, 0·538, 0·6
0·368, 0·6, 0·638, 0·836, 0·86
2·947, 4·279, 7·924, 9·47, 9·7
3·67, 3·68, 3·768, 3·8, 3·867
0·132, 0·213, 0·3, 0·312, 0·32
5·34, 5·354, 5·4, 5·53, 5·543

Now try this!
0·03, 0·3, 0·005

p 30

2·421, 2·425, 2·5, 3, 3·099, 3·4, 3·55
2·789, 2·8, 3·0, 3·725, 3·98, 4·074, 4·462
7·0, 7·567, 7·65, 7·695, 7·765, 7·9, 7·975
8·135, 8·3, 8·315, 8·5, 8·51, 8·513, 8·531

Now try this!
$2 \leq k < 4$
2·421, 2·425, 2·5, 3, 3·099, 3·4, 3·55
2·789, 2·8, 3·0, 3·725, 3·98
$4 \leq k < 6$
4·074, 4·462
$6 \leq k < 8$
7·0, 7·567, 7·65, 7·695, 7·765, 7·9, 7·975
$8 \leq k < 10$
8·135, 8·3, 8·315, 8·5, 8·51, 8·513, 8·531

p 31

0·312	0·337	0·354	0·379	0·393
2·465	2·484	2·508	2·523	2·536
4·81	4·835	4·856	4·88	4·893
6·91	6·938	6·954	6·979	6·993

Now try this!
5·081   5·083   5·086   5·0875   5·0891

p 35

| **1** $\frac{7}{6}$ $1\frac{1}{6}$ | **2** $\frac{13}{10}$ $1\frac{3}{10}$ | **3** $\frac{9}{4}$ $2\frac{1}{4}$ | **4** $\frac{13}{8}$ $1\frac{5}{8}$ |
| **5** $\frac{14}{5}$ $2\frac{4}{5}$ | **6** $\frac{17}{6}$ $2\frac{5}{6}$ | **7** $\frac{27}{10}$ $2\frac{7}{10}$ | **8** $\frac{13}{4}$ $3\frac{1}{4}$ |

Now try this!
$6\frac{1}{3}$ $9\frac{1}{2}$ $7\frac{3}{5}$ $3\frac{4}{5}$

p 36

| **1** $\frac{5}{8}$ | **2** $\frac{3}{4}$ | **3** $\frac{4}{10}$ or $\frac{2}{5}$ | **4** $\frac{5}{6}$ | **5** $\frac{3}{7}$ |
| $1\frac{3}{5}$ | $1\frac{1}{3}$ | $2\frac{1}{2}$ | $1\frac{1}{5}$ | $2\frac{1}{3}$ |

p 37

| **1** $2\frac{1}{7}$ | **2** $4\frac{2}{7}$ | **3** $3\frac{5}{12}$ |

4 $1\frac{6}{12}$ and $1\frac{1}{2}$ **5** $4\frac{6}{12}$ and $4\frac{1}{2}$ **6** $2\frac{12}{24}$ and $2\frac{1}{2}$ **7** $2\frac{1}{6}$

8 $6\frac{5}{7}$ **9** $4\frac{1}{6}$ and $4\frac{2}{12}$ **10** $1\frac{12}{24}$ and $1\frac{1}{2}$

Millie 5 points, Billy 3 points and Lily 7 points.

Now try this!
$4\frac{1}{7}$ weeks $2\frac{5}{12}$ dozen

p 38

1 a	$1\frac{1}{2}$	**b**	$2\frac{1}{4}$	**c**	$2\frac{3}{4}$	**d**	$3\frac{1}{10}$	**e**	$1\frac{1}{5}$
f	$2\frac{9}{10}$	**g**	$1\frac{1}{100}$	**h**	$1\frac{7}{20}$	**i**	$3\frac{2}{5}$	**j**	$2\frac{3}{5}$
2 a	$1\frac{1}{2}$	**b**	$2\frac{1}{10}$	**c**	$1\frac{1}{1000}$	**d**	$1\frac{1}{4}$	**e**	$3\frac{3}{4}$
f	$2\frac{1}{200}$	**g**	$3\frac{1}{5}$	**h**	$1\frac{1}{20}$	**i**	$2\frac{7}{20}$	**j**	$4\frac{3}{5}$

Now try this!

| **a** | $1\frac{1}{2}$ | **b** | $2\frac{1}{4}$ | **c** | $1\frac{3}{4}$ | **d** | $3\frac{1}{10}$ | **e** | $7\frac{1}{2}$ | **f** | $4\frac{1}{5}$ |

p 40

1 $\frac{1}{4}$ 2 $\frac{3}{4}$ 3 $\frac{2}{5}$ 4 $\frac{3}{8}$ 5 $\frac{3}{8}$ 6 $\frac{5}{16}$

7 $\frac{4}{7}$ 8 $\frac{1}{3}$ 9 $\frac{7}{12}$ 10 $\frac{6}{13}$ 11 $\frac{3}{4}$ 12 $\frac{1}{2}$

p 41

1 $\frac{3}{10}$ 2 $\frac{3}{5}$ 3 $\frac{3}{5}$ 4 $\frac{1}{3}$ 5 $\frac{3}{5}$

6 $\frac{3}{7}$ 7 $\frac{1}{2}$ 8 $\frac{1}{3}$ 9 $\frac{1}{3}$ 10 $\frac{2}{5}$

11 $\frac{4}{15}$ 12 $\frac{1}{3}$ 13 $\frac{2}{3}$ 14 $\frac{2}{3}$ 15 $\frac{3}{4}$

Now try this!

$\frac{1}{4}$ $\frac{1}{10}$ $\frac{1}{5}$ $\frac{1}{20}$ $\frac{1}{8}$ $\frac{1}{40}$

$\frac{3}{8}$ $\frac{2}{5}$ $\frac{3}{10}$ $\frac{9}{20}$ $\frac{5}{8}$ $\frac{19}{20}$

p 42

$\frac{2}{3}$ yellow: $\frac{14}{21}, \frac{18}{27}, \frac{10}{15}, \frac{100}{150}, \frac{20}{30}, \frac{60}{90}, \frac{30}{45}, \frac{32}{48}, \frac{40}{60}$

$\frac{3}{4}$ red: $\frac{9}{12}, \frac{30}{40}, \frac{15}{20}, \frac{75}{100}, \frac{21}{28}, \frac{45}{60}$

$\frac{4}{5}$ blue: $\frac{8}{10}, \frac{20}{25}, \frac{28}{35}, \frac{128}{160}, \frac{48}{60}, \frac{16}{20}, \frac{80}{100}, \frac{160}{200}$

$\frac{7}{10}$ orange: $\frac{35}{50}, \frac{56}{80}, \frac{49}{70}, \frac{28}{40}, \frac{14}{20}, \frac{21}{30}, \frac{42}{60}$

$\frac{5}{8}$ green: $\frac{40}{64}, \frac{50}{80}, \frac{30}{48}, \frac{55}{88}, \frac{25}{40}, \frac{250}{400}$

p 44

1. BAC 2. BCA 3. CBA 4. ACB 5. ABC 6. BAC

p 45

CHOMP   CRAWL   SHINY   BLACK   BEAST

p 46

45 mins, 30 mins, 9 mins, 42 mins, 44 mins, 20 mins, 26 mins, 3 mins, 10 mins, 15 mins, 24 mins, 18 mins, 40 mins

$\frac{3}{60}, \frac{3}{20}, \frac{1}{6}, \frac{1}{4}, \frac{3}{10}, \frac{1}{3}, \frac{2}{5}, \frac{13}{30}, \frac{1}{2}, \frac{2}{3}, \frac{7}{10}, \frac{11}{15}, \frac{3}{4}$

Now try this!

$\frac{1}{6}, \frac{7}{24}, \frac{1}{2}, \frac{5}{8}, \frac{2}{3}, \frac{3}{4}, \frac{5}{6}, \frac{11}{12}$

p 49

Two out of five

p 50

84%, 80%, 84%, 95%, 86%, 80%, 75%, 90%, 96%, 90%, 84%, 87%, 30%, 90%, 90%, 91%

p 52

| 40% | $\frac{2}{5}$ | $\frac{40}{100}$ | $\frac{4}{10}$ | | | 60% | $\frac{3}{5}$ | $\frac{30}{50}$ | $\frac{6}{10}$ | $\frac{60}{100}$ |

75% $\frac{18}{24}$ $\frac{3}{4}$ $\frac{12}{16}$ $\frac{9}{12}$ $\frac{6}{8}$ **15%** $\frac{15}{100}$ $\frac{3}{20}$

90% $\frac{9}{10}$ $\frac{18}{20}$ $\frac{90}{100}$ $\frac{45}{50}$ **25%** $\frac{1}{4}$ $\frac{5}{20}$ $\frac{15}{60}$ $\frac{8}{32}$ $\frac{25}{100}$

35% $\frac{7}{20}$ $\frac{35}{100}$ **64%** $\frac{32}{50}$ $\frac{128}{200}$ $\frac{16}{25}$ $\frac{64}{100}$

p 53

1 3 shapes blue

2 4 shapes yellow and 1 red

3 7 shapes green and 2 blue

4 6 shapes yellow, 3 red and 4 green

5 3 shapes green and 1 red

6 9 shapes blue, 1 red and 7 yellow

7 2 shapes blue, 6 red and 10 yellow

8 11 shapes red, 24 yellow and 1 blue

9 1 shape green, 4 yellow and 7 red

Now try this!

1 25% 2 50% 3 10% 4 35% 5 20%

6 15% 7 28% 8 28% 9 52%

p 55

1 a 40 hundredths, $\frac{40}{100}$ or $\frac{4}{10}$, $\frac{2}{5}$ 25 hundredths, $\frac{25}{100}$, $\frac{1}{4}$

c 5 hundredths, $\frac{5}{100}$, $\frac{1}{20}$ d 4 hundredths, $\frac{4}{100}$, $\frac{1}{25}$

e 6 tenths or 60 hundredths, $\frac{60}{100}$ or $\frac{6}{10}$, $\frac{3}{5}$

f 68 hundredths, $\frac{68}{100}$, $\frac{17}{25}$

2 a 0·4 b 0·25 c 0·05 d 0·04 e 0·6 f 0·68

p 57

1 a 42 b 14 c 63 d 91 e 105 f 77

2 a 6 b 10 c 14 d 8 e 16 f 24

Now try this!

a 8 b 12 c 24

  28   42   84

p 60

1 a £1.80 b £1.60 c 60p d 55p

e 90p f £2 g £5.40 h £3.85

i £4.50 j £7.60 k £1.50 l £7.15

2 a 400 g b 300 g c 200 g d 300 g

e 250 g f 250 g g 225 g h 1000 g

i 125 g j 175 g k 325 g l 450 g

Now try this!

0.6p   0.8p   1.2p   1.1p

p 61

1 40 km 2 45 km 3 48 km 4 50 km 5 54 km

Now try this!

a 120 km, 135 km, 144 km, 150 km, 162 km

b 60 km, 67·5 km, 72 km, 75 km, 81 km

p 62

1	225 g	2	8	3	420 g
	270 g		960 g		490 g
	450 ml		160 g		140 g
	126 ml		16		245 g
	9		1120 g		7
			720 g		259 g

Now try this!

1	250 g	2	10	3	600 g
	300 g		1200 g		700 g
	500 ml		200 ml		200 g
	140 ml		20		350 g
	10		1400 g		10
			900 g		370 g